The
FALL
of the
ALPHAS

The
FALL
of the
ALPHAS

THE NEW BETA WAY TO CONNECT,

COLLABORATE, INFLUENCE—AND LEAD

DANA ARDI

ST. MARTIN'S PRESS
NEW YORK

www.stmartins.com

Library of Congress Cataloging-in-Publication Data

Ardi, Dana.
  The fall of the alphas : the new beta way to connect, collaborate, influence—and lead / Dr. Dana Ardi. — First edition.
      pages cm.
  ISBN 978-0-312-68193-7 (hardcover)
  ISBN 978-1-250-03812-8 (e-book)
  1. Organizational change. 2. Organizational behavior. 3. Organizational effectiveness. 4. Corporate culture. 5. Leadership. I. Title.
  HD58.8.A736 2013
  658.4'06—dc23   2013014167

First Edition: October 2013

10 9 8 7 6 5 4 3 2 1

This book is dedicated to my parents,
FAY and JACK SILVERSTEIN

and to my beloved Grandmother
IDA GORDON SCHACHT

CONTENTS

INTRODUCTION: A Tale of Two Cultures   1

ONE: Corporate Anthropology   11

TWO: Plows and Primates   52

THREE: Boomers and Bonobos   66

FOUR: Information Changes Everything   79

FIVE: Communication, Collaboration, and Curation   89

SIX: The Top of a Different Pyramid   123

SEVEN: Eliminating Elitism   140

EIGHT: Managing Ego   161

NINE: It Takes Two to Beta   188

TEN: Chasing Mentors and Motivated Skills   201

Epilogue   209
Acknowledgments   211
Endnotes   213
Index   217

A TALE OF TWO CULTURES

It was the best of times, it was the worst of times, it was the age of wisdom, it was the age of foolishness, it was the epoch of belief, it was the epoch of incredulity, it was the season of Light, it was the season of Darkness, it was the spring of hope, it was the winter of despair, we had everything before us, we had nothing before us, we were all going direct to heaven, we were all going direct the other way—

—CHARLES DICKENS, *A Tale of Two Cities*

Today's American corporate world is a tale of two cultures. One, more traditional and common, is centralized and hierarchical. I call it *Alpha*. The other, smaller and rarer, is decentralized, horizontal, and inclusive. I call this one *Beta*. Probably the best way to understand their differences would be to observe the two, side by side. Doing so in the real world is physically impossible, and doing so in this book would only result in a tedious series of case studies. Instead, let me take you with me on hypothetical visits to a pair of representative companies, and describe what I see and hear (or don't see and don't hear) that helps me characterize them as either Alpha or Beta.

We begin our tour with an imaginary media company, headquartered in a major metropolitan area. It's located in a new building in a posh, up-and-coming neighborhood filled with other gleaming corporate towers.

Since the neighborhood is relatively new and composed primarily of high-rise buildings, it's noticeably lacking in small businesses such as restaurants, bars, diners, grocery stores, or dry cleaners. Instead of sidewalk food carts, a small number of licensed kiosks provide food, drinks, and snacks. Enormous plazas designed for public use surround the office buildings. Cars, trucks, and all incoming deliveries are funneled discreetly into underground garages. There's a nearby bus stop and train station.

The ground floor of the media company consists of a towering atrium lobby with a trickling waterfall on one side. Elevators lead to a mezzanine level dotted with smaller suites, most of which belong to doctors, lawyers, and accountants. To board the elevators that take you to the highest floors of the office tower, you need to navigate not one but two security checkpoints. To my right is a bank of local elevators that make stops at most floors. To my left are the express elevators that whisk visitors to a handful of high floors, all of which house the most senior leadership of the tenant firms.

Even though it's the morning rush, and the right-side elevator bank is teeming with sharply dressed, coffee-toting men and women, the express elevator that takes me up to the CEO's office is empty. When the doors slide open onto the twenty-sixth floor, I cross over into a seating area of matching chesterfield couches, across from which is an imposing wooden dais with the company's name emblazoned on the front. Behind the dais sit two stylish, well-coiffed women and two no-nonsense-looking men, the latter pair sporting short-cropped-bordering-on-Navy-SEAL haircuts. On the walls behind them is artwork depicting the company's numerous media properties, from cable TV to Web sites to radio stations to newspapers and magazines to broadband service.

After greeting me, one of the women asks me to take a seat as I wait for someone to guide me to the CEO's office. It's clear this is the default protocol for everyone, including employees, who also require a guide to escort them back into the inner sanctum. Directly inside the imposing wooden doors is a second sitting area whose furniture and décor precisely match the setup of the outer lobby, including an identical set of chesterfield couches. Surrounding each area are four scaled-down versions of the outer lobby dais. A woman stands behind each dais, her job being to usher visitors from the outer lobby to this inner lobby. Just as before, I'm invited to take a seat, and five minutes later, a young man who introduces himself as the CEO's executive assistant leads me back to the appropriate office.

Inside the CEO's suite, I'm walked through a cluster of linked cubicles that adjoin four rooms: a restroom, a coffee room complete with a fridge and microwave, a technology center with printers and copiers, and a conference lounge with a round table and four chairs. The CEO's office dominates one entire corner of the floor. My guide opens the door and announces my name.

The CEO rises from behind the glass Bauhaus-style desk and we shake hands. She appears to be in her mid-fifties, and her perfectly fitted, basic black suit is understated and elegant. She motions me over to one of the three Le Corbusier chairs arrayed in front of her desk before retaking her own seat.

Let's call the CEO Sherri Rosen. In anticipation of our meeting, naturally I'd done my due diligence. A graduate of one of the Seven Sisters, with a degree in communications, Sherri went on to get her MBA at an Ivy League university. She started off her career as a successful marketing executive for a book publisher, and then became CEO of a start-up specialty cable channel. Her success there led to her being recruited to take the CEO spot at this enormous multichannel media organization.

Sherri explains that she's seeking advice in recruiting staff and management for the company's recently created digital media division. In describing what exactly she is looking for, Sherri focuses on the efforts and personalities of the new executive vice-president who heads the digital division and of the veteran head of the company's human resources department. As I keep probing for information, I discover that the digital VP works in one of the adjoining office suites, alongside the VPs in charge of the company's broadcast and print divisions and the other "C-level" executives. The HR executive works on a different floor altogether.

After getting an informal sense of the structure of the organization and a taste of its culture, I ask to meet the new digital VP. It turns out he's not in the office that day, so his assistant sets up a meeting between the two of us later that week. Next I ask for a tour of the offices of the new digital division. At first Sherri suggests that her executive assistant serve as my guide, but very gently I request that she show me around the offices herself. "It will make a difference," I say.

As we make our way to the internal stairway that connects the executive floor to the other floors, Sherri points out the dining room and conference room that are reserved exclusively for the officers who toil on the executive floor. Up the staircase and emerging onto another level, all of a sudden I'm confronted by a radically different floor plan, this one made up of a giant, endless labyrinth of workstations. Interspersed among the cubicles are various coffee/lunch areas, while restrooms and technical rooms surround the stairs and the elevators. Small, enclosed offices curl around the outside walls, and every single corner is dominated by a glass-walled conference room.

Sherri's executive assistant accompanies us every step of the way, discreetly keeping everybody on course. Based on the reactions of the employees in the cubicles, it's obvious that a CEO walkabout isn't an everyday occurrence. The word ripples through the floor: *The boss is here.* At one point, Sherri pauses in front of a cubicle in the digital division area. Glancing at the plaque on the wall, Sheri introduces me to the employee sitting there, then asks the clearly rattled young woman to tell me exactly what she does. Haltingly, the young woman proceeds to offer up a novice-level description of her responsibilities as a Web site designer, using terms like *graphic interface* and *hypertext*. When I ask her to tell me more about the company, I can't help but notice she uses the word *great!* a lot.

After a few more similarly uncomfortable meet-and-greets, I ask to meet the head of human resources. His office is on yet another floor, one similar in design and atmosphere to the one we just left. A distinguished-looking man in his early sixties, he's taken aback but not flustered by our unscheduled appearance, and seems eager to discuss recruiting strategies and tactics. When I ask that Sherri, her executive assistant, and the head of the digital division also sit in on the meeting, the CEO looks surprised. So does her assistant, who suggests we assemble in the executive conference room. I successfully press for an off-site meeting instead.

Now let's pay a visit to the second hypothetical company, this one an outdoor equipment company that sells exclusively online. The company has its headquarters in a sprawling single-story building in an underpopulated region on the outskirts of a college town.

Because it's a rural setting, there are no other businesses nearby. The company's glass-and-steel building sits on a parklike setting, with hiking and biking trails winding through fields, streams, ponds, and stands of trees. There's a large parking lot about a quarter mile from the building itself, with a minibus shuttle that goes back and forth from the lot to the main building. The parking lot abuts a pair of tennis courts and a basketball court. There's a municipal bus stop in front of the building itself.

A young man posted at a lectern just inside the door greets me when I enter. Wearing a wireless headset and wielding a tablet computer, he introduces himself, asks my name, and invites me to take a look around while I wait for my host, the CEO of the company, to arrive.

In the lobby behind us is a series of market-style stalls housing a dry cleaner and a small drugstore satellite, as well as a number of food vendors. Directly across the lobby is a day care center, a well-equipped gym such as you'd find in a hotel, and a cafeteria offering a limited, healthy menu. From what I can see, the rest of the building appears to be a haphazard collection of individual workstations, large and small conference areas and equipment hubs filled with printers, copiers, whiteboards, microwaves, coffeemakers, and refrigerators.

There's no discernible pattern to how the people here appear to be interacting. Some are working on their own, while others are operating in small teams. To a man or a woman, the employees seem relaxed but purposeful. Noticing a stranger in the building, many nod or smile or say hello, and a couple stop to ask if I'm lost and can they help me? Just then Jim Campbell, the CEO, shows up.

As usual, I had spent a couple of weeks before my visit researching the company and its leaders. Jim is a graduate of the nearby university and he combined a computer design education with a passion for the outdoors in founding his company, which is now five years old. He started his career by working first for a retail cooperative, and then for a large outdoor equipment manufacturer. Along the way, he developed a design for an ergonomic, electronics-friendly backpack that attracted the attention of some angel investors, whose seed money enabled him to launch his business. Based on how he's dressed, it's hard to distinguish Jim from his employees. In fact, as far as I can tell, each employee is dressed in chinos or jeans, sneakers or hiking shoes, and one of four different-colored tennis shirts embossed with the company's logo. In my pressed business suit, I'm feeling slightly overdressed.

Jim gives me a quick tour of the premises, taking especial pride in the cafeteria, whose chef is an old college friend who once ran a local vegetarian restaurant. Next, he leads me to his workplace. Instead of a glass-walled corner office, Jim runs his company out of a centrally located workstation no different from any of the others in the building (though I have to say it's messier than most). He introduces me to his executive assistant, Claire, who's hard at work at an adjacent workstation, and the three of us make our way to a nearby round table.

As Claire sets up her laptop and I set down my briefcase, Jim takes coffee orders, then disappears to fetch us the drinks. Once he returns, he pulls up a chair and explains the reason for our meeting. It seems the company's pack and bag business has been extremely successful, but Jim and his management team believe the company needs to add a line of more fashionable products for "urban adventurers," in his words. Problem is, neither he nor his current staffers know enough about that market to supervise the development and rollout of a new product line. Jim also strongly believes the design and marketing team for the new line should be located in an urban environment. That way, the surroundings can influence the team's work just as the current team draws inspiration from living and working in a country setting. The second issue? Jim is nervous that the company's current culture won't translate to an urban workforce and environment. Which is where I come in. Can I help Jim and his team define and clarify the existing culture, and develop ways his team can apply it to a different place and population?

With this mission in mind, I ask Jim to tell me more about his executive team and the company's overall structure. Immediately Claire pulls up an organization chart on her laptop. Rather than an organizational model that looks like a tree, it's a collection of individual hub-and-spoke charts with interconnected lines. "I like to joke that the chart changes so often that no one here ever bothers printing it out," Jim says. After all, the company is made up of project and product teams of designers, marketers, and salespeople. Some people work on more than one team; others work on just one. The only group that seems semipermanent consists of HR, Finance, and IT, and is internally dubbed "Support Team."

After taking in all this information, I ask Jim if he'd be willing to take me on a tour of the premises. Claire politely bows out, leaving Jim as my sole guide. Together, we wind our way through assorted workstations and conference areas. The only organized element of the floor plan, so far as I can tell, is a number of intersecting "hallways" marked by red tape on the floor that are clear of any furniture and equipment, and that lead to exit doors.

Few employees take any special notice of the CEO as Jim shepherds me through the company. Those who do greet him by name, and ask about this or that product or initiative. In turn, Jim not only seems to know everyone's name, but he also appears familiar with whatever issues they bring to his attention. Before long, we run into David, the company's chief strategist, whom Jim has named to head up the project team in charge of developing plans for the new product line. David tells me that the entire project team consists of four people: himself, the head of HR, a marketing colleague who's willing to relocate to an urban setting, and a designer who had done the opposite, by relocating from a metropolitan area to take a job here with Jim's company.

We set up a meeting two weeks hence, at which time I'll present them with some ideas.

As Jim walks me back to the lobby, he invites me to come back later that afternoon for a company outing. I'm sorely tempted and wish my schedule allowed it, but instead I head home.

Now, obviously I've used some hyperbole to emphasize the differing behaviors, environments, and cultures between these two completely invented companies. But these contrasts encompass the wide range of difference I encounter regularly in my business. I spend a great deal of my daily work life studying, understanding, diagnosing, and helping repair the core cultures of organizations. That's because I'm a corporate anthropologist.

ONE

CORPORATE ANTHROPOLOGY

I wear power ties, I tell power lies, I take power naps,
I run victory laps. I'm a totally ongoing bigfoot slam dunk rainmaker
with a proactive outreach. A raging workaholic; a working rageaholic.
Out of rehab, and in denial. I've got a personal trainer,
a personal shopper, a personal assistant, and a personal agenda.
You can't shut me up, you can't dumb me down. 'Cause I'm tireless,
and I'm wireless, I'm an alpha male on beta blockers.

—GEORGE CARLIN, *Life Is Worth Losing*

For thousands of years, groups of people have looked to a single strongman for leadership. Families had patriarchs. Tribes had chieftains. Villages had lords. Nations had kings, prime ministers, presidents. Over time, this ancient model defined by one powerful figure dominating the rest of the group has been applied to practically every sphere where groups of individuals work together. Cities have mayors. Armies have generals. Teams have quarterbacks. Nuclear families have fathers. And corporations have CEOs. In the 1940s, we came up with a catchall description for this ubiquitous archetype. We dubbed these strongmen *Alpha males,* a term we borrowed from studies of the animal world.

For all of prehistory, human societies were egalitarian, collaborative communities of hunters and gatherers. The typically male role of hunter wasn't valued any more or any less than the typically female role of gatherer. Both provided sustenance for the tribe. In fact, considering that females were the source of life itself, societies revered matriarchs as much as they did patriarchs. It wasn't until the development of agriculture and the necessity of being able to plow for crops that physically stronger males began to dominate. The adoption of agriculture also meant that tribes became rooted, rather than nomadic. In turn, fixed locations led to greater population density and heightened competition—competition, I might add, that led to hierarchical rather than collaborative group dynamics.

When society morphed from the Agricultural Age to the Industrial Age, the leadership paradigm failed to evolve along with it. In fact, during the Industrial Age, the Alpha model became even more ingrained. Although working on an assembly line did not require physical strength, labor became firmly divided along gender lines. Men worked outside the home; women worked inside the home. If circumstances obliged females to seek outside employment, they did so in roles that mirrored their by-now-customary roles: cook, maid, laundress, seamstress. For most of the Industrial Age, in fact, the only professions that welcomed females were those requiring the role of nurturer: teacher and nurse.

In the 1980s, when women began to collapse gender barriers and occasionally assume an exalted profesional status, they were dubbed *Alpha females*. This very minor tweaking of the name made sense, considering that the behaviors and attitudes of many Alpha women were indistinguishable from men heading up similar groups. Many of these women had decided that the only way they could succeed professionally was by becoming exactly like men. They surrendered most vestiges of their femininity. They desexualized themselves. The wore tailored shirts and even female neckties that both mimicked and parodied a traditional male wardrobe. Books from that 1980s era had titles like *Games Mother Never Taught You:*

Corporate Gamesmanship for Women, which counseled women entering the workplace to avoid any and all so-called subservient positions. Among other things, women were advised never to take notes, as their colleagues might then perceive them as secretarial. (Today, I'm constantly reminding young women of the power inherent in minutes-taking. The way I see it, aggregating the sum of organizational data is about as far as you can get from subservience!)

Again, women who rose to top positions in the 1980s and 1990s felt almost as though they had to out-Alpha the Alpha male. They not only had to be aggressive and tough but they also had to be twice as aggressive and tough as all the men out there. Think of empire-builders Martha Stewart or Linda Wachner, the CEO of apparel giant Warnaco. Wachner rose from working as a department store buyer to leading a leveraged buyout of the global company she would eventually lead. She soon quadrupled the size of Warnaco's business, which owned numerous high-end brands including Calvin Klein jeans, Ralph Lauren Chaps, Speedo swimwear, and Olga bras.

Like numerous Alpha men before her, Wachner was ultimately brought down by her own hard-charging management style. She was, the word went, too abrasive, too critical, too autocratic. She drove away key management talent. She didn't heed the advice and counsel of subordinates. Most unforgivable to stakeholders, under her governance Warnaco began hemorrhaging money, and ultimately filed for bankruptcy protection in 2001. That same year, Warnaco fired Wachner without severance pay.

Author Sarah Dunant was once quoted as saying, "[The] Alpha female, like [the] alpha male, depends on such a state of innate superiority that she's probably not aware of her status. While she would be effortlessly talented and capable, she would need a reduced capacity for empathy, because otherwise it would derail her. . . . I envisage the mind of Mary Warnock, the body of Kate Moss and the humanity of Leni Riefenstahl."[1]

"[The] Alpha female is pretty exceptional," agrees UK *Guardian* columnist Polly Toynbee. "There are not a lot of people trying to be like her, whereas there are a lot of men behaving in the same way, clambering over each other to reach the top of the tree. Those women who do get to the top are mavericks, hybrids and deny that they are like other women. Women do not like the Alpha female very much, nor do they want to be like her. Women want to be liked, which holds them back," Toynbee concludes, adding that English Prime Minister Margaret Thatcher was the only female leader in history whose cabinet lacked even a single female.[2]

Whether male or female, an Alpha is an Alpha, right?

So why did the Alpha model of business leadership and its hierarchical organizational structure last as long and spread as wide as it did? Because it worked, that's why. The risk-taking, competitive, self-assured boss was lauded for his or her decisiveness, certainty, and willingness to go it alone. Was he or she disagreeable? Occasionally. Callous and insensitive? Sometimes. Close-minded and obstinate? Often. But those negative traits were condoned, accepted, and even admired as part of what it took to reach the top dog slot and lead the group to success. Moreover, an Alpha leadership style worked best with a carefully structured pyramid of support beneath it. There needed to be a clear hierarchy, or chain of command, usually divided up into functional branches, in which people knew their roles, carried out orders from above, and in turn gave orders to those below them. For the next generation of leaders, there was only one clearly marked path of ascension or leadership to follow, and only one sharply defined set of skills for them to possess: the path that led to the CEO job, as well as to the huge, glassed-in corner office.

No doubt about it: this historical, hierarchical Alpha paradigm had a heralded, unprecedented run. For thousands of years, it was the model for nearly every group of human beings, from the Roman Empire to 1950s America, from Patton's Third Army to Jack Welch's General Electric to Tom Brady's New England Patriots. It was the traditional way to lead a company, structure an organization, and run a family. But everything comes to an end.

The generations that came of age in the 1970s and 1980s saw themselves as rebels. They were ahistorical and antiestablishment. The civil rights, women's rights, and gay rights movements all had their origins in the youth-based counterculture that flowered during those two decades. The irony was that gender roles and the Alpha paradigm were as firmly entrenched in these "revolutionaries" as they were for previous generations. What *was* revolutionary, however, was how this generation grew up to raise their own children. Those young people, who have grown up to become today's knowledge workers, weren't necessarily forced into strict gender roles, and growing up, they also learned that every member of the team had a valuable role to play. In short, most were taught to be true to themselves *and* to work well with others.

Eventually, when they graduated from college, these young people found themselves entering a new kind of economy: the Information Age. In the Industrial Age, work was algorithmic and incremental. Experience mattered more than anything else. This made it a natural fit for the hierarchical Alpha structure and leadership paradigm. By contrast, work in the Information Age is heuristic—it stimulates inquiry, oftentimes by trial and error— and fluid. Creativity matters more than experience, since, let's face it, today memory can be digitized. The sheer ubiquity of information and instantaneous communication has given a generation that feels entitled to speaking its mind the ability and the means to call out opinions twenty-four hours a day, seven days a week. Information technology has also led to the globalization of economies and cultures. Today's businesses no longer exist in a closed system. No one leader can have all the answers, nor can any stand-alone leader ignore the power of today's new 24/7 information flow. This combination of information and communications technology has brought down more despots than all the smart bombs built over the course of the Industrial Age. Hierarchical organizations, in which decision-making is centralized in one person, or within a small, elite group of people, are becoming as obsolete in today's world as political autocracies.

Which is another way of saying that the future belongs to the Betas, not the Alphas, and to organizations and leaders who communicate, collaborate, and curate.

Information is now so valuable and so widespread that trying to keep it under control isn't only counterproductive, it's also bound to fail. Today's organizations and leaders must have as open a dialogue as possible, not just internally, with employees, but also externally, to the public, and in some cases, the world.

As everyone knows, information technology has made the world vastly more complex than it used to be, and it continues to do so in leaps and bounds. It is impossible for one person, no matter how brilliant or dynamic he or she is, to master all the knowledge a company needs to compete. In the Information Age, success requires leaders who are willing and able to collaborate with employees, directors, customers, and competitors.

Which is where Beta comes in.

Beta leaders and employees are fully networked into their communities. They influence rather than intimidate. They play to their strengths and seek help from others to compensate for whatever skills they lack. Rather than aspiring to omnipotence and acting as though they're the masters of all they survey, Beta leaders focus on what I call *motivated skills*, for example, the things they know they do exceptionally well. And instead of exploiting their peers' weaknesses in order to attain and hold on to power, they encourage their fellow executives to play to *their* own strengths so that the entire team and organization can succeed.

For a leader, this requires the ability to curate—to listen and to guide—rather than command. The ideas, products, and efforts of all the organization's constituents must be woven together into a cohesive narrative. And those individuals who work in Beta organizations must be encouraged to pursue their own areas of interest and expertise, rather than forcing themselves to follow a culturally preapproved development path.

Which is where the Beta leader steps in. He or she understands that every individual in the organization is a contributor; the closer everyone in the organization comes to achieving his or her singular potential, the more successful the business will be. Beta leaders encourage their employees to acquire new skills, but rather than responding to a company mandate, employees *themselves* set out to expand their skill sets. In the Beta organization, individual development is all about self-actualization, as opposed to self-promotion.

Now, self-actualization doesn't mean slinging a backpack over your shoulder and spending six months beachcombing the sands of Costa Rica. It's more accurately defined as self-awareness. Beta companies generally encourage employees to bring to their roles an intellectual and emotional understanding of their strengths and their weaknesses, their goals and their motivations. And among the qualities that make up successful Beta leaders is a willingness to help employees reach a high level of awareness via self-directed learning—which is one reason why the 360 reviews (performance-appraisal data collected from all around an employee) and feedback sessions in many corporate offices seldom have any teeth. (I'm a long-standing believer in self-directed learning, with an encouraging assist from the top.) Leaders need to give their people the proper tools, techniques, and feedback. At the same time, organizations cannot be wholeheartedly responsible for their employees' development; employees have to play their parts, too.

For example, if an executive says to an employee, *You are unbelievably good at doing* X, *but less adept at doing* Y, *and I'd like to help you develop your skills at* Y *with the following techniques and protocols,* well, to me that's a conversation that's actually liable to bear fruit. Another executive might tell an employee, *You're a really incredible VP of Marketing, but you lack equally great financial modeling skills. To that end, we recommend that you consider pursuing an executive MBA. Oh, and one more thing? We're not going to push you toward doing that, but we will support you every step of the way, and make a long-term commitment not just to your continuing education, but to your role in this company as well.* Which is why among the characteristics that define Beta leaders and organizations is the ability to imbue employees with processes designed to make them better than they are, and that help them play to their strengths and shore up their weaknesses.

Whether they're executives or directors, today's most successful Beta leaders apply the same principles to their organizations' development as they do to their own, and their employees', development. Just as Alphas build hierarchical organizations, Beta leaders create horizontal organizations that mirror their own approach to collaboration and teamwork. Beta companies are communities, not armies. They are made up of shifting, project- or process-based teams instead of rigid functional silos. On one project someone might take on a leadership role, while on the next that person will be just another team member. Instead of following individualistic, ego-driven tactics designed to meet quarterly numbers and boost short-term revenue (and compensation), Beta executives and directors pursue strategies that benefit the entire community through growth and long-term profitability. The successful corporate leadership of today evolves the company toward its own kind of self-actualization; of becoming the best at what it does best.

Example: What does a company like Apple do best? The short answer would be "Whatever it wants," but in 2001, when Apple decided to expand its brand into retail, few industry observers predicted the experiment would work. Today, there are 326 Apple stores across the United States, Europe, and Asia, which in 2010 accounted for roughly $3 billion in sales.[3] As *The Wall Street Journal* points out, "More people now visit Apple's 326 stores in a single quarter than the 60 million who visited Walt Disney's four biggest theme parks last year."[4] As the world's most valuable company, one many experts believe may someday become the world's first $1 trillion business, Apple holds an enormous share of the fast-growing smartphone market (especially across emerging markets) and a near-monopoly on music downloads. The company produces the default MP3 music player for all ages in the iPod, and has a 54 percent market share in the tablet market. Sure, the company sells desktop and laptop computers, but what Apple is really selling is style, simplicity, beauty, high-tech design, and treasurelike packaging, while inspiring in its customers a reverence more typically associated with religion. (When I recently visited the standing-room-only flagship Apple store in Midtown Manhattan, it looked and felt like an international day care, while only half a block away, FAO Schwarz, the world-famous toy store, was nearly empty.)

Facebook is another enormously successful company that is sticking to what it does best: being the world's best, most influential targeted advertising platform. The numbers speak for themselves. More than one in thirteen people on earth today have a Facebook account. Facebook users spend over 700 billion minutes every month on the site. Every twenty-four hours those users install 20 million apps, and every month some 250 million people engage with the site from outside Facebook's official Web site, meaning, via mobile phones and tablets. Half of all individuals under the age of thirty-five rely on Facebook as their exclusive source of news gathering. And as any casual user probably already suspects, Facebook has become the largest photo-sharing album on earth. But in the face of its IPO, has Facebook announced plans to expand its services into providing content, or creating its own proprietary games? No. At least for now, Facebook will continue playing to its unparalleled strengths by bringing people together and further buttressing its position as the most powerful advertising platform in the world.

Finally, Amazon.com may have evolved into a digital version of a Greek agora by discounting everything from kids' toys to rug shampoo to beauty products to lawn mowers to digital cameras, but most consumers still associate the online retailer with books and reading. Strangely enough, founder, president, and CEO Jeff Bezos was a computer science major in college with little interest in books and authors. But in 1994, during the first iteration of dot-com mania, Bezos studied the top-20 mail order businesses and wondered, *Which of these industries could the Internet handle more efficiently, profitably, and on a much larger scale?* Bezos chose books. The rest is history, as Amazon began sharply underselling the prices set by publishers and bricks-and-mortar bookshops. In 2007, reversing the marketing strategy known as the "razor and blades business model," whereby a company sells an inexpensive platform, then charges customers high maintenance fees (think of the prices of shaving razors, or how much it costs to replace the ink in your printer), Amazon began manufacturing the world's first-ever e-book reader, the Kindle, and began selling electronic versions of books and magazines at a loss to ensure it became the dominant player in the e-book category.

Bezos and his team recognized a few things that traditional publishers were slow to acknowledge. The first was that in an impatient, impulsive Information Age, customers expected instant gratification. (Amazon whizzes e-books to an e-reader in seconds.)

Second, Amazon realized that books were beyond the price range of many consumers. Yet in discounted, electronic, ten-dollar versions, readers could be tempted to take risks on new authors and unknown titles when they weren't willing to take on writers or books that were retailing for three times that amount. Finally, synchronous with a wobbling global economy and a growing focus on environmental issues, many consumers were doing away with extraneous clutter—and that included old books. Today, five or so years after Amazon's entry into digital publishing, the company's e-book sales make up roughly two-thirds of the total e-book sales in the United States. Not least, Amazon had created a new distribution model for writers who are today able to bypass traditional routes— the literary agent and the publisher—and publish their books via "backdoor" methods.

Amazon hasn't stopped there. In 2011, the company launched its own publishing platform, setting the company up to compete directly with traditional New York publishers. Led by a former publishing executive, Amazon has already signed up several high-profile writers, helping them develop content while offering the company's own in-house marketing and delivery system. It also rolled out "Amazon Singles"—original articles that range in length from five thousand to thirty thousand words that the company sells for anywhere from $0.99 to $2.99, and that can earn Singles authors including Stephen King, Lee Child, Amy Tan, and Ann Patchett a roughly 70 percent royalty rate. The Singles program has been so successful that Amazon can almost be credited with inventing a new genre that straddles a universe in between a very short book and a stretched-out piece of journalism.

Assertive Alpha-style leadership isn't extinct. There's a bit of the autocrat and control freak inside every successful entrepreneur. Ego and assertiveness are no doubt necessary for someone to be able to buck the odds and successfully bring his or her idée fixe to fruition. And in times of crisis, existing companies typically find there's no replacement for the speed and clarity that come from having a single decision-maker at the helm.

The terrorist attacks of 9/11 caused most businesses to recalibrate their priorities, and find ways to slice money from their operating budgets. I was working in private equity at the time. In the days after 9/11, I remember that our entire team took a serious, big-picture view of all our businesses. We asked ourselves the tough questions: *How can we preserve jobs, conserve our energies and resources, and evolve in the weeks, months, and years ahead?* In the end, rather than telling our top people in every company division to chop 20 percent of their operating budgets, which is how many Alpha companies responded in the months after 9/11, our approach was inclusive. There were no top-down mandates or across-the-board eliminations. Instead, we formed a committee to figure out the best possible solutions, and asked everyone in the organization for his or her input. During the 2008 economic downturn, one Beta company I know of encouraged all hands to step up and take responsibility and ownership of the company—and ended up eliminating not jobs, and not employees, but of all things, *snacks.* You read that right. The team asked itself: *Would you rather have peanuts 24/7 or jobs?* In the end, the company did away with the cookies, popcorn, and tubs of Cup-a-Soup that had previously been available at all hours to all employees. Instead of firing people, or decimating division budgets, the powers-that-be replaced the commissary with vending machines. Company employees were so relieved to hold on to their jobs that I doubt they missed the free 24/7 peanuts and pretzels.

September 11, 2001, also gave Jimmy Dunne, the CEO of investment banking firm Sandler O'Neill & Partners, an opportunity to reset his company's priorities. Sandler O'Neill's offices were on the 104th floor of the World Trade Center, and when the planes crashed, of the eighty-three company employees at work that day, sixty-six died. According to *Fortune* magazine, Sandler ultimately lost 40 percent of its employees, including "a third of its partners, all its bond traders, its entire syndicate desk and almost all its equity desk."[5] The next day, CEO Dunne put on his sharpest Brooks Brothers suit and addressed his employees. He, the firm, and the nation were in the midst of an unimaginable national tragedy, he told them. He understood if any of his employees wanted to go home, change jobs, or even change careers. Ultimately, most of his people stayed put, relieved to be able to funnel their fear, anger, and grief into productivity. Six days later, when the financial markets reopened, Sandler O'Neill had reopened its doors in a small Midtown office. By the end of the year, the firm was once again profitable.

On 9/11, countless Beta leaders came forward to take control of the crisis. JetBlue, the discount airline, was founded in 2000 by Brazilian-born entrepreneur, David Neeleman. Neeleman's mission was to restore not only quality but also humanity to an industry where cramped seating and high prices were the norm, and where customers typically came last. JetBlue's culture put a premium on fun, passion, integrity, informality, and outstanding service. Passengers making phone reservations were more likely to find themselves talking to a stay-at-home mom in Salt Lake City than to be put on hold by a tightly scripted sales associate. From the beginning, Neeleman also made it clear that every JetBlue employee was a "crew member," from the pilots to the vice-presidents to the men and women who tossed your suitcase onto the luggage carousel. No matter who you were, JetBlue expected you to roll up your sleeves, grab a vaccuum cleaner and a trash can, and help clean the airplane in preparation for the next flight out.

JetBlue was one of our portfolio companies back in the days when I was working in private equity. Then 9/11 happened. That day, all flights were grounded. I lost count of the number of people who told me they would never board an airplane again. Many experts went on record as saying that the airline industry would never recover.

In the wake of 9/11, one of the very first calls we received was from JetBlue. Could I help the airliner find a new, permanent Head of Security? The next morning, Neeleman appeared on NBC's *Today Show* to reasssure the American public that his airline had just bought a new fleet of planes equipped with armored cockpit doors with titanium locks. JetBlue had also installed cabin camera surveillance systems that permitted the pilot and the cabin crew to see what was happening on the plane at all times.

In Neeleman's *Today Show* appearance was a near-perfect example of a leader of a Beta company taking charge during a time of national upheaval. (Calling someone a "Beta" in no way suggests that he or she is not a leader—in fact, as we'll see, nothing could be further from the truth.) Over the next few weeks, as the airline industry continued its financial slide, JetBlue's pilots union voluntarily offered to take a pay cut as a demonstration both of company loyalty and admiration for how Neeleman was steering them through catastrophe. JetBlue recovered and, then as now, has extraordinarily high popularity and customer satisfaction ratings.

Only six years later, Neeleman stepped up again, this time during a PR disaster of JetBlue's own creation. It was Valentine's Day, 2007. An ice storm had caused numerous tarmac delays at New York's JFK Airport. Most airlines canceled all incoming and outgoing flights and told passengers to go home and reschedule their travel plans. JetBlue opted to stick things out. Big mistake. Thanks in part to a breakdown in the airline's communications system, hundreds of passengers found themselves stranded on JetBlue's planes for six hours or more. Over a seventy-two-hour period, nearly a thousand JetBlue flights were canceled. Tempers raged to the point where police had to be called in. At which point, CEO Neeleman came forward to acknowledge, and apologize for, his company's miscalculations. A week later, JetBlue went so far as to roll out a customer bill of rights that guaranteed its passengers free or reduced-fare flights and cash incentives if they ever found themselves stranded on a tarmac again. The offer was retroactive to Valentine's Day. It's worth noting that later that same year, airline passengers again ranked JetBlue number one in customer satisfaction in areas ranging from on-time performance to in-flight service. Today, Neeleman is no longer the company CEO, but JetBlue is still profitable, and despite pressures from outside organizers, crew members have opted not to unionize.

It doesn't take a national catastrophe, or freak weather conditions, to impel a leader to step up to the plate. Leadership also involves shepherding a business forward while taking note of challenges and trends that might endanger the future and profitability of that business. Consider the decision that Richard Harrington, then-CEO of the Thomson Corporation, one of the world's largest publishers, made in the late 1990s to divest the company of its core newspaper publishing business.

What led to Harrington's decision? While chatting with a car dealer during a ski vacation, the CEO gleaned that consumers were now coming into this man's car dealerships armed with pricing information they had gleaned from the Internet. An interesting insight? Sure. One that most people would have tucked away and forgotten about. But Harrington had the beginning of an epiphany. If consumers were scouring the Web before they bought cars, didn't that suggest that newspaper advertising—the basis of newsprint revenue—would soon be migrating online, too?

The CEO had a hard decision to make. The Thomson Corporation—today known as Thomson Reuters—was built on the back of newspaper publishing, and owned 250 newspapers across the globe. At the time the company was also immensely profitable. But Harrington heeded what his gut was telling him. He drilled down deep on industry knowledge and growth forecasts, as well as on subscriber and consumer data. What he found confirmed what he already knew, and in the months ahead, Harrington made the bold move to sell off Thomson's entire newspaper business. The decision paid off spectacularly. Today, according to several estimates, newspaper revenue from classified advertising, including automotive and real estate, is roughly one-tenth of what it was in 2000.

The long-term success of both new and existing companies requires abandoning the old Alpha leadership and structural model and adopting the Beta paradigm.

Building a Beta organization, and becoming a Beta leader, requires changing ingrained attitudes and behaviors that have been associated with business leadership almost forever.

I'm not saying it's easy—only that it's essential! The process starts by changing your focus from one pyramid to another. Beta leaders work at reaching the top of Maslow's Hierarchy of Needs pyramid, rather than the top of an organization's Hierarchy of Titles pyramid. For Beta leaders, self-actualization, which comes from self-awareness, combined with a deep-seated understanding of your strengths and your weaknesses, matters far more than self-promotion. Moreover, the employees in a Beta organization must be encouraged to make the same shift.

Practically and symbolically, elitism must be eliminated as much as possible for an organization to succeed and thrive. Status perks like executive parking spots and executive dining rooms should be replaced by Employee of the Month parking spots and corporate cafeterias. Instead of focusing on people who have the best metrics, companies need to recognize the facilitators within the organization, while "craftspeople" need to be as valued and rewarded as managers.

Finally, Beta leaders need to practice ego management. They need to be aware of their own biases, and focus as much on the present as on the future. Beta leaders need to manage the egos of employees by rewarding collaborative behavior and teamwork. Beta leaders must become what Michael Maccoby coined Productive Narcissists,* tempering high self-esteem and confidence with empathy and compassion. Mindfulness, of self and others, by executives and employees, may very well be the single most important characteristic of a successful company.

Many high-profile organizations make it a point to cherry-pick potential candidates from a small number of top-ranked colleges and universities. These candidates tend to be highly motivated, driven people. All their lives they have strived—or been pushed by their parents—to excel and to win. They have followed a seemingly predestined road map laying out what they or their families believe they should do to get ahead in the world. Seldom have most of them bothered to pursue an interest beyond those that will help them rise to the top. Are they highly individualistic? Quirky? Transgressive? Have they ever tried something, failed at it, and instead of beating themselves up, said to themselves, "Huh. That was no good. What can I learn from having messed up?" In most cases, I doubt it.

This is among the many downsides of considering only candidates from "branded" colleges and universities. Thanks to stepped-up competition for an increasingly limited number of slots, these institutions have lost whatever alchemical ability they once had to transform a student's promise or potential into something greater. Nowadays, top-ranked colleges are obliged to accept entire incoming classes of uncommonly ambitious, accomplished students and then, four years later, graduate even more exaggerated, entitled

---

* Michael Maccoby, *The Productive Narcissist: The Promise and Peril of Visionary Leadership* (New York: Broadway Books, 2003).

versions of those same students. So where does that leave most of us?

Hallmark, the giant card company, was one of the very first companies to leverage the idea that quirky, angular employees *matter,* and should be welcomed, courted, and celebrated—that they actually made the company what it was. Hallmark has also long believed that innovation, creativity, and creative renewal are team sports. In the mid-1990s, the card company attracted a great deal of media attention thanks to the mini-sabbaticals, or "rotations," that it offered its seven hundred employees, who produce roughly twenty-one thousand designs yearly.[6] How did Hallmark keep its employees motivated and on-task? By creating a large, off-campus "innovation facility" that offers classes and workshops in everything from engraving to leather tooling, and by transforming a nearby farmhouse into an artists' studio. Hallmark employees could also immerse themselves in half-year-long rotations where they could explore a contemporary social trend, for example, religion or ethnicity. The company's only mandate was that employees had to share what they learned with their colleagues. These "mini-sabbaticals" weren't just intriguing company perks. They were key in helping Hallmark employees broaden the scope and intimacy of their card lines and rededicate themselves to the company's mission and bottom line.

These days, numerous businesses, including Pixar, carry out contemporary variations of Hallmark's "farm" concept. As the company behind animated movie hits like *Toy Story, Finding Nemo, Ratatouille,* and *Wall-E,* Pixar has long been an organization that celebrates angular thinkers, even misfits. It's also a company whose culture is practically underwritten by innovative teamwork and collaboration. At Pixar's northern California offices, skilled employees across all divisions work in teams, with veterans working alongside new hires. Instead of titles, rankings, and caste systems based on status, pay, title, and importance, Pixar workers are defined by the skills they bring to the organization, whether they're artists, programmers, screenwriters, or senior executives. In short, Pixar is all about teamwork, and the courting and sparking of countless free-form ideas. Company president Edwin Catmull once said famously, "A mediocre team will screw up a good idea. But if you give a mediocre idea to a great team and let them work together, they'll find a way to succeed."[7] The company even operates its own in-house Pixar University, made up of over a hundred different classes ranging from theatrical improv to sculpture to line drawing to creative writing.

Google is another company whose leaders go out of their way to encourage employee innovation. Like Pixar, Google encourages its engineers to spend 20 percent of their time focusing on their own ideas and innovations. As *The Washington Post* points out, "Many of the personal projects yield public offerings, such as the social networking Web site, Orkut, and Google News."[8] Richard Holden, a Google product management director, says, "If you're not failing enough, you're not trying hard enough. . . . The stigma [for failure] is less [at Google] because we staff projects leanly and encourage them to just move, move, move. If it doesn't work, move on."[9] How then does Google make hiring decisions? Think college admissions, real-world division. Is the person a good fit, that is, is the applicant untraditional, a little wild, a little indescribable, in short "Googley"? Says Laszlo Bock, Google's vice-president of People Operations, "We skew toward people who like to solve problems—the bigger the problem, the better, rather than those who settle in and say, 'Okay, I'll do that for 30 years.'"[10]

SAS, the North Carolina–based, privately held software giant, also believes in making its employees happy. The company must be doing something right. SAS has a 98 percent customer renewal rate, and a roughly 3 percent turnover rate among its ten thousand-plus employees, who enjoy thirty-five-hour workweeks, unlimited sick leave, no-cost on-site health care, a gymnasium, discounted country club memberships and, on Wednesday, as many free M&M's as they can eat. Says CEO Jim Goodnight, "M&M's have become something of an icon representing SAS's corporate culture, but that was just a fun tradition we hung onto over the years. . . . It represents a mindset we have. From the earliest days of the company, we wanted to create an environment similar to the university, where you have the freedom and flexibility to be creative."[11] Asked why more companies fail to make the connection between employee satisfaction and higher productivity and profits, Goodnight said, "They only see employee benefits as costs that show up on the balance sheet. . . . Because we put employee-oriented measures in place long ago, we have the benefit of years of experience to show that the long-term benefits far outweigh the short-term costs. Most companies don't know how to represent that kind of return in their annual reports."[12]

Which goes to a point that author Alison Hemming made in a blog post following the publication of Greg Smith's widely circulated 2012 *New York Times* op-ed disparaging the corporate culture of his employer, Goldman Sachs. Today, Hemming notes, the best talent have no interest in spending their lives in a single cubicle. Instead, these men and women are actively managing their own careers. Today's workers invariably have a professional Plan B, thanks to the personal and professional network they've created via LinkedIn, Facebook, and other sites. "Talent wants partnership, not ownership," Hemming writes. "And an esprit de corps that they can believe in. Give it to them, and they'll reward you with their ideas, great work, and a lifetime relationship. Doing nothing will lead to a brain drain of epic proportions that will make you feel like Kodak or Yahoo on a good day."[13]

Or why not try integrating storytelling into your workplace culture? Russell Goldsmith, the chairman and chief executive of

City National Bank in Los Angeles, says that stories are "a really important part of how we teach and reinforce the culture, and how we reward behavior."[14] City National Bank goes so far as to bring in consultants who teach employees how to organize stories in a way that highlights what is best about the company culture. In a nod to *American Idol*, Goldsmith says, "We do something called 'Story Idol,' and every quarter there's a competition among our seventy-nine offices. It's a way to give colleagues a pat on the back and a moment in the sun for doing the right thing, and it democratizes and decentralizes positive reinforcement. We then have a Story Idol competition for the year in a big meeting with the top 300 people in the company. People tell stories about what they did that promoted teamwork or helped a client by going the extra mile. It's like telling stories around a campfire, but they're doing it around conference tables."[15] City National Bank employees submit anywhere from fifty to one hundred stories per quarter, which show up on the company's intranet—and then every employee votes for the winners. The people who submit the winning stories receive iPads. The employees singled out for helping clients get large cash awards. Adds Goldsmith, "But what matters most is the recognition, and the respect from your peers as you stand on the stage in front of 300 people."[16]

Even a national supermarket chain can create an in-house enthusiasm that ensures both employee loyalty and strong financial returns (and in an industry with fairly slender profit margins, too). Frequently cited by *Fortune* magazine as among the best companies to work for in America, Wegmans is a privately held supermarket chain with seventy or so stores in the Northeast. The company's hourly wages and salaries exceed the industry standard, and Wegmans has spent tens of millions of dollars over the past two decades providing college scholarships to both full- and part-time employees. Operating on the belief that no customer should leave a

Wegmans supermarket unhappy, employees are tasked to do everything short of massage therapy to ensure this happens. Wegmans is also more or less flat in its structure. *Fortune* notes that when one Wegmans supervisor asked an employee to analyze a rival's shopper-loyalty program, the employee ended up discussing her findings directly with company president Robert Wegman.[17] Now, *that's* what I call a Beta organization.

From where I sit, among the most interesting things about "new economy" companies—whether they are start-ups across the food industry, the health-care industry, or the information industry—is the increasing number that are being built on a venture capital model of shared equity, meaning that every employee earns a portion of the company's overall revenues. Sure, employees in these new start-ups tend to work their tails off, but at the end of the day they also have an equity stake in the company's financial future. (Many larger companies have tried to duplicate this model by rewarding individuals, or whole divisions, an approach that hasn't worked nearly as effectively.) Today, I'm glad to report that in many start-ups I counsel, the venture capital model comes with the territory. Search firms, consulting firms, advertising agencies, and even law firms are all rewarding hard work and collaborative behavior.

Recently I sat down with a female executive at a global advertising agency. Her mission, she told me, was to bring together teams to collaborate on individual brands, and reward them for the quality of their work. By "rewarding" them, she wasn't talking exclusively about money, either. Rewards can include everything from encouraging employees to work on their own pet projects to developing new products and services. Some companies even ask their employees: *How can we help you develop and expand your career?* And many, as we've seen, are creating in-house incubators for younger talent. This is a future trend worth watching and emulating. By now, you may have guessed that if you *don't* reward your employees, chances are high they will jump to a company that actively supports their growth and future development.

Of course, the model of employees having a financial stake in a company would be incomplete without mentioning the wacky example of an artist present at the creation of an Internet phenomenon. In 2005, Sean Parker, then president of a fledgling online company known as Facebook, offered a young Korean American painter and graffiti artist named David Choe the sum of $60,000 in exchange for painting a few murals on the company's northern California office walls. Or, Choe could opt instead for company stock. Choe chose the stock. Six years later, when Facebook announced plans for its IPO, overnight Choe was worth anywhere from between $200 million and $600 million. Oh, and his murals still decorate Facebook's company walls today.

To my mind, the very best way to visualize the differences beteen the Alpha and Beta approaches is to contrast a general and his army to a conductor of a symphony orchestra.

The Alpha leader and organization is the general and his army. Underneath our hypothetical Alpha general are four colonels: one in command of infantry, one in command of artillery, one in command of cavalry, and one in command of overall logistics. Underneath each of those colonels are two majors, each in charge of one division of their colonel's branches. Underneath each of the eight majors are two captains. Underneath each of the sixteen captains are two lieutenants. And underneath each of the thirty-two lieutenants are two sergeants. Finally, every single one of those sixty-four sergeants leads, oh, let's say, approximately a dozen soldiers.

The general draws up his own plan of battle, perhaps soliciting advice from his four colonels, perhaps not. He issues his orders to those four, which they then pass down the chain of command. The majors no doubt have some sense of the big picture, and might be able to whisper an idea in their colonels' ears, but otherwise, they have practically no role in the plan. Forget about the 640 soldiers. Their opinions don't count. As far as their own advancement is concerned, the paths are stratified and strict. An officer moves one rank at a time, inside his own branch. A captain of artillery can only become a major of artillery. He'll never be able to jump to the cavalry.

Now: Replace those four branches with management, marketing, finance, and sales, and the colonels with executive vice-presidents, and you've got a pretty good snapshot of the traditional Alpha business structure: a single decision-maker, function-based organizational silos, tunnel vision, and formally defined career paths.

By contrast, the Beta leader and organization more closely resemble a conductor of a symphony orchestra. The orchestra is also divided up, but into instrumental sections rather than functions. There are woodwinds, brass, percussion, and strings. Although each section has a leader, those leaders are not in command. They serve as mentors, and now and again they may step forward as soloists. And rather than the rest of the section falling into a stratified hierarchy, every player is a member of a team that works in synchrony.

Even though the conductor may direct the actions of the orchestra, they are not the sole planner. The composer writes the music. And a featured soloist may provide his or her own interpretation of the music. Meanwhile, instead of issuing commands, the conductor strives to get the various groups working together to produce a memorable performance. Her goal is to get the members of the orchestra to play to the best of their ability, while integrating those efforts into a unified group effort. There are times, let's say, when playing Vivaldi, when the string section predominates. At other times, maybe while playing Purcell, the horns are front and center. The technical demands of musicianship are so great that it's rare for a musician to make the leap from one instrumental section to another. But a conductor can come from any section of the orchestra, or none at all. What's more, a skilled performer doesn't feel any pressure to trade up and become an orchestra leader. Joshua Bell can focus on being one of the best violinists in the world without thinking or being told that to truly succeed in the classical music world, he needs to become the next Leopold Stokowski or Leonard Bernstein.

Next: Replace woodwinds, brass, percussion, and strings with engineering, design, marketing, and sales, and you have an intimate portrait of the modern Beta organization: planning and ideas originating from a number of sources, a collaborative effort facilitated by the leader, no single route to leadership, and no pressure to become anything other than the very best at what you do.

To my mind, the Beta model isn't just a prescription for business success. It also offers an opportunity to be truer to our own human natures. The fact is, most of us aren't Alphas; we're Betas. In our hypothetical Alpha Army, there are 765 people, and of those, only a few aspire to becoming a general. Even in our hypothetical eighty-member-strong Beta Orchestra, probably only a couple of them harbor dreams of someday conducting the orchestra. We'd all be happier not being someone we're not, even if society has told us since we were born that we're meant to aspire to the gold medal, and the winner's circle. Most of us want to accomplish things in our lives, but few of us are driven to dominate others. We know there are things we do exceptionally well, and things we do less well. There are times we want to take the lead, and other times when we're happy contributing, assisting, listening, facilitating, and even cheering other people on from the sidelines. Most of us are satisfied with the opportunity to accomplish what we're good at, and what we enjoy, so long as we receive adequate recognition and reward— which doesn't necessarily mean we want to become the CEO or the leader. And if we *do* harbor corner-office ambitions, few of us are comfortable with ruling over others like an absolute monarch.

If I had one piece of advice for today's knowledge workers, it is this: It's okay to be yourself. It's laudable, in fact, to be skilled at what you do best, whether it's marketing, finance, telecommunications, human resources, publishing, or raising your children. Ambition and the human desire for status and money, are natural and normal. But ambition can be horizontal as well as vertical. Employees don't always have to move *up*. Employees can also move *across*. Being Betas simply means that most of us do not necessarily set our sights on rulership, or on becoming the CEO. Beta means that we are, or should be, content where we are professionally, that our ambitions should lie in the realm of self-awareness and self-improvement, and that we shouldn't feel we have missed the boat if we do not aspire to lead, dominate, or become the sole decision-maker. The Beta movement is about excellence, achievement, and success. It is about finding happiness and fulfillment in a career where you develop yourself, contribute to the community, and feel productive. What it is *not* about is becoming someone you are not, and feeling diminished as a result even though you are perfectly content with the intrinsic and extrinsic rewards of your job.

I once counseled the chief financial officer of a major division of a large film studio in Los Angeles. Let's call him "Sam." I'll never forget the day I first caught sight of his office suite. He had not one, not two, but three receptionists, and a huge corner office that came with a decorating budget. A casual visitor would tell you that Sam—a young Alpha male with money, power, position, and status—had everything going for him. On the surface, he did, too. Yet Sam was unhappy and frustrated dealing with the studio hierarchy, and spent his days worrying he was going to make a mistake and take a fall. As we got deeper into our conversation, it became clear that in spite of the job perks, Sam was stuck. His job didn't allow him to flex his entrepreneurial muscles, or satisfy his true passion, which was new technology. He felt isolated, alone, and vulnerable.

It so happened that I knew about a job opening in an emerging technology company that was growing and scaling. On a hunch, I told Sam that he should at least consider applying for it, and I ultimately made the match and placed him there. A few months later, Sam and I ran into each other by accident in an airport. Well, "ran into" doesn't quite describe our encounter. Sam literally grabbed me by the shirt, and with an enormous smile on his face, told me that I had ruined his life. He had taken the job, and was now working for the emerging technology company. He no longer had three receptionists at his beck and call. He shared one assistant with three other suite-mates. He poured his own coffee. Gone was the dramatic office with its view of downtown Los Angeles and the Pacific. His new digs were cramped and windowless and since the company was still in its frugal, venture-backed early days, Sam was on an airplane in a coach seat most of the week. Instead of Armani suits, his new wardrobe was a dress shirt and jeans. Yes, he missed the perks of his old job—who wouldn't?—and he had never been busier, but he loved his new job, and he loved his new life. We said good-bye. A few months later, Sam was named the company's COO, and when the company went public two years later, his personal windfall came to around $70 million. Today, Sam is a venture capitalist and angel investor helping other entrepreneurs and young companies attain their dreams.

As one of the three founders of Twitter, Evan Williams is another businessman who stepped down from an Alpha position—the CEO of Twitter—to take a company role that better fit his strengths. As everyone knows, Twitter has rechoreographed the way users exchange real-time information, and along with Facebook, has played a profound role on the global political arena. But in 2010, Williams decided he would cede the Twitter CEO position to Twitter's then-COO, Dick Costolo. Williams would retain his place on the board; after all, without him, there would be no

Twitter. But rather than spending his days dealing with administrative tasks, he would devote the rest of his career at the company to product development.

What drove his decision? Self-awareness. Williams was famously skilled at figuring out the needs of new technology users, and he had helped scale Twitter from 5 million registered users to 71.3 million users.[18] He was far less at home carrying out the micromanagerial and administrative duties that the CEO position demanded. It is a truism of the business world that the person who launches a business is often not the best candidate to scale that business at various critical junctures of its growth. Williams knew he'd made mistakes as a CEO, and that Costolo was as obvious a candidate as any to make the company even bigger and better than it was. Today, Twitter is thriving both domestically and overseas. As for Evan Williams, he spends his days focusing on new product development. He is a person who embodies the advice I give to people to play to their strengths or, as I like to put it, "Stick to your knitting, baby."

Then there's David Pottruck, the CEO of financial services colossus Charles Schwab, who was promoted to the top spot in 2003 after serving for five years as co-CEO alongside firm founder Charles Schwab. In the summer of 2004, the company was in a stubborn holding pattern. The stock price was flat. Employees were being laid off. When Pottruck showed up for work, Charles Schwab told him that the board had lost confidence in the direction the company was headed, and that he, Schwab, was retaking the CEO position, and Pottruck was out. Now, many CEOs in Pottruck's position might have taken this public beheading as an opportunity to retire, and many have. Instead, Pottruck launched a new company called Red Eagle Ventures, while wrestling with the thought that he had to be—or rather, *should* be—a CEO in the financial services industry again. But as time went on, Pottruck recalled how many things about being CEO he had disliked, from the Black-Berry tethered to his wrist, to the tedious, time-consuming administrative tasks, to the long meetings, to how little time he was able to spend with his wife and children.

Recalling how much happier he was at Charles Scwab when the firm was smaller and more daring, and wondering whether he just might be happier not as a CEO but as a company chairman, Pottruck began to explore positions in newer, more nimble companies. In a speech he delivered to students at the University of Pennsylvania's Wharton School of Business, Pottruck was candid: "It's new to me to be an ex-CEO. . . . My leaving Schwab was on less than elegant terms. It was a pretty humbling experience for me. It wasn't humbling because I was replaced. . . . What is really humbling is to have time to reflect on what you've done and what you could have done better."[19] The students gave him a standing ovation.

Pottruck began a gradual professional reinvention. He took a hard look at everything he had done right and wrong at Charles Schwab. He had been a micromanager who now and again created unnecessary bottlenecks at the top. He hadn't done enough careful strategic planning. He had focused on far too many initiatives. He hadn't taken the time or the trouble to develop his relationship with the board. Now it was time to learn from his mistakes and move forward. In 2005, Pottruck became the chairman of an airline start-up, Eos Industries, and today, alongside his duties at Red Eagle, he also serves as cochairman of Chicago-based wealth-management firm, HighTower Advisors. Sure, there are things he misses about the CEO role at Charles Schwab, but his new positions give him everything he wants.

The Beta model has also trickled down to our personal lives. The family model of *Leave It to Beaver* and *Father Knows Best* now seems almost Jurassic. Even the super-achieving, two-income Huxtables of *The Cosby Show* now seem obsolete. Today, we're more like the couples in *Modern Family*. That popular TV show features an older man living with a much younger woman and her son; a stay-at-home mom and working dad with three children; and a gay couple rearing an adopted Asian child. Our neighborhoods are full of stay-at-home dads, blended families, single parents, gay and lesbian couples raising children, and every other imaginable variation. Decision-making is collaborative. At any point, parents swap "stay at home" and "go to work" roles, just as they could both enter or retire from the workforce. What matters isn't that the heads of households follow a traditionally defined pattern, but that they do what works best for their families.

That said, the Alpha family model still haunts many late baby boomers today. Dad hunted; Mom gathered; Dad was the boss, the authority; Mom was the organizer, the detail person, the glue who kept daily life intact and running. But even men and women who were reared in so-called traditional households find that that Alpha paradigm no longer works. Or if it does, that the traditional titles mother and father bear little relationship to contemporary reality.

I know several couples where the wife works, and the husband stays home. This can happen for various reasons: the woman has a soaring career, say, while the man is in a creative industry. I know of one man who cannot match his wife's earning potential, and thus the two of them have decided it makes greater economic sense for her to work, and for him to care for the children and manage the home. But even in families where both partners leave for work every morning, the Beta marriage of today is fluid, improvisational, and nonhierarchical. Depending on where you live, it is almost the norm.

Richard, a male advertising executive in his late-forties, always assumed that when he married and had children, he'd be the Alpha. His father, after all, was the stern, authoritative type, while his mother was a homemaker. When Richard and his wife, Ellen, had the first of their two children, his professional life didn't change much, either. He still commuted to work every morning, came home at six, played with the kids, and worked late into the night on his laptop. Whereas Ellen, a psychotherapist, put aside her career to become a full-time mother. She took their three children to day care, to music lessons, to medical appointments, to playdates and sleepovers, while also doing most of the cooking, cleaning, and housework.

But as time went on, Richard and Ellen began to discover innate talents and abilities they didn't know they had. Gender had next to nothing to do with it. There were things Richard did better than Ellen, and things she did better than he did. Unexpected things, too.

Take budgeting. Richard had always paid the bills. But with his workload stepping up, he surrendered that role to his far more efficient, practical wife. As a former college jock, Ellen got a kick out of taking her son to soccer practice in the afternoons. Richard had always loved to cook and work around the house. And in spite of his work schedule, he began preparing his children's box lunches early in the morning while he fixed coffee for his wife.

In short, in that family, you couldn't tell who was the Alpha and who was the Beta. Why? Because both Richard and Ellen were Betas *as well as* Alphas, dialing up and dialing down their strengths and skills as circumstances demanded. When Ellen eventually returned to work part-time, Richard reconfigured his own schedule so he could be at home the two mornings a week when she was heading to the office. He shuttled the kids to school, did the family acquisitioning, and in the afternoons, when Ellen and their son were at soccer practice, he escorted his two daughters to their dance class. Richard and Ellen's marriage is a genuine partnership. And my guess is that with a rapidly increasing number of women in today's workforce, traditional gender roles will continue to become more and more flexible, elastic, and—no surprises here—more satisfying to both parties.

I realize that promoting the Beta paradigm as a model for business success, personal fulfillment, and family happiness is something of a grand pronouncement. Yet I don't make this pronouncement lightly. Beta isn't the result of a midnight epiphany, or a last-second conversion. It's the fruit of more than two decades of working in and for large organizations, and bringing to that work a somewhat singular perspective.

As I mentioned earlier, I think of my role as akin to a corporate anthropologist. Which means I spend my days studying the cultures of organizations, how they grow and develop, and how the people in them influence and shape their communities. In the very same way a traditional anthropologist might study a Central Asian agricultural community in its natural environment, I study contemporary business people in their natural environment: the workplace.

That might sound esoteric and academic, especially when coupled with my having a Ph.D. after my name. But I've actually spent most of my adult life in the corporate world, which, admittedly, wasn't the original plan.

When I was young, I was profoundly affected by seeing William Gibson's *Miracle Worker* on Broadway. It wasn't the performance of Patty Duke, playing Helen Keller, that touched me the most; it was Anne Bancroft's portrayal of Annie Sullivan. Sullivan was a woman who worked hard to address the needs of a severely handicapped child, while at the same time helping the family of that child reorganize itself around Helen's capabilities. Sullivan was a coach, a mentor, an influencer, and a transformer. She was the figure who ignited my own earliest ambitions. She was also a great role model for a Beta leader: helping others become who they were meant to be.

After college I went to work as a community organizer during the early days of the community mental health movement. At the same time, I was doing academic research on the changing images of handicapped children in the media. After getting my doctorate, I took a position teaching Special Education in the Graduate School of Education at Fordham University. Even though I enjoyed teaching, I recognized that my greatest talent was for bringing about successful social and economic transformations in communities. Eventually, I decided to take that talent to the business world.

I left Fordham University to become president of the Infotainment Corporation, where I consulted for leading studios and publishers, as well as for technology, retail, and telecommunications companies. I then became senior vice-president of new media for RR Donnelley, & Sons Company. From there I moved to TMP Worldwide, where I served as co-chair of the company's Global Communications Entertainment and Technology practice. I spent the next two years at Flatiron Partners, where I worked on human capital issues with early-stage companies. I then joined J.P. Morgan Partners, then CCMP Capital private equity partnerships, where I served as a venture catalyst, creating the structures of organizations, building high-caliber teams, and providing ongoing counsel.

In time, I decided I needed to create my own business devoted to helping people realize their potentials through work. Behind that shift was the influence and inspiration of another extraordinary woman.

My grandmother came to this country from Russia when she was sixteen. She arrived holding the hand of her five-year-old brother. The two of them were the only survivors of a family of thirteen siblings; the others were killed during an attack on their village. They were taken in by an American relative who, it turned out, saw in my teenaged grandmother a source of free labor.

Treated like a domestic rather than as a member of the family, my grandmother realized she'd have to take responsibility for herself and her younger brother. Among her daily chores was shopping. She convinced the owner of the local grocery store to hire her, and from that day forward, she and her brother worked in and lived above the store. Eventually, my grandmother and the shopkeeper's son married, and they adopted her little brother (who later grew up to become a well-known New York physician).

Soon after their marriage, my grandmother and grandfather began helping immigrants adjust to their life in this country. My grandparents provided many new arrivals with a good meal, clothes, money, and the help they needed to tap into networks that could help them succeed. In her own way, my grandmother was as much a model of Beta leadership as Annie Sullivan: they both found fulfillment by helping others reach their potential. By the time she died, my grandmother had helped more than five hundred people from all over the world establish themselves in America. People traveled from across the country to attend her funeral, pay their respects, and tell their stories. Hearing those people testify at her funeral inspired me to build a career in which I could do the same.

Shortly after her death, I launched my own consulting company. I specialized in transforming businesses and human capital, coaching executives in building skills, attracting top-level talent, and designing their ideal organizational structures. In the corporate world, I wanted to accomplish something similar to what my grandmother had done in her own community: give people the tools to achieve their highest potential. I wanted to bring the kind of community organizing I'd done early on in my career to the faster-paced business world. And so my company, Corporate Anthropology, was born. I knew one thing for certain: that by studying in depth an organizational community and culture the way an anthropologist looks at a residential community, business leaders could create healthier, more productive environments.

Soon, though, my idealism came face-to-face with reality. When I began meeting clients, most had only one thing on their minds: leadership. Few executives seemed interested in the corporate community as a whole; or whether or not employees were happy, satisfied, or productive. No inside employee, nor any of the outside consultants brought into most organizations, paid much attention to the hundreds or even thousands of "non-leaders" who made those companies run. Instead, they focused solely on the "top dogs."

The consequences were obvious—that is, if you were willing to look closely. I discovered there was rarely any sense of community in these organizations. Employees didn't know what skills or talents their colleagues brought to their jobs, where their colleagues lived, or, for that matter, whether they had families or children. Almost all my conversations with employees focused on an impossible or intimidating boss, or a snarky, undermining coworker. No one talked about the organization as an organism, or said, "I love my job." The typical workplace was largely if not entirely defined by power, control, status, authority, and money.

This was mirrored in the spooky homogeneity of many workplaces' floor plans. An ornate corner office for the boss, smaller offices for the senior management team, and look-alike cubicles for the people who carried out the day-to-day work. A not-so-well-hidden message was conveyed: Employees are undeserving of any privacy, and almost nothing they say matters. Many times I'd walk through cubicle arrays alongside CEOs who had seldom navigated those areas before. "This is Mary," they'd say, having quickly scanned the nameplate on the cubicle. "Mary does all our merchandising plans. Mary, tell Dr. D about your work." Mary, who'd probably never come this close to the CEO before except in a bad dream, would fidget and squirm before launching into an anxious, improvised soliloquy.

During every one of these early coaching projects, I'd try to expand the conversation so I could figure out how the place as a whole operated. Business organizations can be compared to natural systems, like marshes or wetlands, in which everyone and everything connects. In a healthy organization, as in a productive natural system, every individual has a place and the entire organism works together in synchrony. In an unhealthy system, one species dominates, cutting off the growth and evolution of the others, creating a domino effect of imbalances. Invariably, whenever I asked executives and employees to sum up the culture of their organization, they would use one word over and over: *great. But if everything was so great,* I kept asking, *why did you call me in here?* Repeatedly I'd push to try to get the insights I needed. In return I'd be told, bluntly, "There's no need to explore that. We just need to fill this position," or words to that effect. The team, community, and shared goals of the company were irrelevant. The executives were interested in their organization's *egoSystem*, not its ecoSystem."

Whenever I coached private clients, I ran into equally disillusioning situations. One month really stood out and it stays with me to this day. I was called in to counsel an executive who had been acknowledged as the CEO-in-Waiting of an enormous high-tech company. The current CEO, who planned to retire in the near future, had recruited this executive and, with the board's approval, given him responsibility for running day-to-day operations while the current CEO focused on external business development. Together, the two men formed an effective, efficient partnership. Ironically, because the partnership was so productive, the current CEO reconsidered his retirement and, with the board's agreement, decided to stay on after all.

In our initial meeting, the CEO-in-Waiting expressed his anger, frustration, and feelings of betrayal. He told me he was afraid he'd now never reach the top spot in the company, and that his reputation would be damaged if he was no longer seen by others as next in line. As a result, he wanted to leave the company and restart his ascent to the top elsewhere.

A week later, another client came to me with the same problem, and the same frustrations. This time, it was a vice-president of marketing who felt stifled by the head of her division. She'd been given performance goals, but couldn't get the appropriate resources or approval from her boss. Her two peers in sales and product development were under equal pressure. These three executives were working against each other to achieve individual goals, rather than in tandem to achieve mutual goals. And their division head was doing nothing whatsoever to ease the competition and ensure the levers of success.

The marketing vice-president felt handcuffed. She knew how to get the results, but no one was letting her. The only way she could get what she needed was by playing the kind of company politics she abhorred, and winning at the expense of her colleagues. When we spoke, she was debating whether to make an end run around the division head, or start looking for another job.

The weekend after my meeting with the marketing vice-president, I spent a couple of hours on the phone with the son of a good friend. I'd been asked to give some career guidance to this young man, who'd been working as an in-house designer for several years. A bright, creative, ambitious young man in his early thirties, he spent most of our conversation telling me about the shortcomings and failings of his supervisor, the art director. My friend's son maintained he was more creative and prolific than his boss, and better at bringing clients' ideas to life. Apparently, the only area where the art director topped him was in his take-home pay. My friend's son loved what he was doing. He loved the company. In fact, he loved pretty much everything about his work, except for one thing: He wasn't running the show.

That month's worth of sessions served as an illustration and microcosm of what I'd observed in my years of executive coaching. Despite being at very different phases of their careers, working in different industries, for very different companies, and facing dissimilar situations, almost everyone I'd met with was frustrated by their inability to be the top person. It seemed to me that the root cause of their unhappiness wasn't a mercurial or demanding CEO, a manipulative division head, or an overachieving art director. No, the source of everyone's unhappiness was a corporate culture in which shared goals and collaborative teamwork had no place. There was no such thing as "community," it seemed; offices were little more than spaces shared by a group of rabid competitors. Everyone I spoke with felt like a contestant on *Survivor*.

Just as I was beginning to wonder whether I could bring my anthropological approach to the corporate world and to individuals, I began working with information-economy start-ups created by groups of twenty-something men and women: GeoCities, which eventually turned into Yahoo; AOL, back in its early, pre–Time Warner days; The Street; Return Path; and many other venture-backed start-ups. It was the receptive audience I'd been waiting for.

These organizations were already on their way to becoming the kind of communities I'd spent years promoting. They were Beta companies. They were horizontal rather than hierarchical. Individuals didn't feel compelled to climb a corporate ladder to feel successful or satisfied. Employees didn't follow conventional patterns. They focused instead on collaboration and teamwork. Needless to say, this new landscape was exhilarating. These were kinetic, dressed-down environments where employees created their own miniature collectives. During morning meetings and at lunch, almost everyone working there had an idea or initiative he or she was willing to toss out. Roles, identities, and responsibilities mutated weekly, sometimes daily. *Leadership* was a loose and elastic term.

There was talk of social, global, and environmental responsibility. These young knowledge workers seemed willing and eager to try out and develop new concepts rather than slavishly follow the rhythms or fiats of traditional roles and structures.

What made these knowledge industry start-ups even more intriguing was that every single one of these businesses was successful—and growing fast. In other words, these collaborative communities weren't just good for their people, they were great for business, too. Here was a concept, even a movement, that I could sell to other clients: that leading in a wholly new way, and building a wholly new kind of company—a collaborative community of shared responsibility—could dramatically boost revenues.

I was thrilled to find companies that embodied the values that I'd been preaching. My discovery led me to hunt down more examples I could show to new clients, and I've been finding them ever since. Many were start-ups, but there were also existing businesses that had evolved from Alpha to Beta. And not all of them were in the high-tech world, either. Timberland, The Container Store, Green Mountain Coffee, Starbucks, and Whole Foods were among the best known organizations that had been practicing and moving to the Beta model for years.

In my practice as a corporate anthropologist, I now had positive examples I could point to if clients ever expressed reluctance or trepidation. I began focusing on what I could do to bring the collaborative horizontal ethos to business environments that were stuck in competitive hierarchical mind-sets. My goal wasn't, and still isn't, to transform established, successful, conservative companies. Rather, it's to help organizations position themselves to succeed with today's workers, and in today's new business environment. I may refer to the meetings I use to brainstorm as Tribal Councils, but any resistance from the skeptical "chief" and the company's "elders" goes out the window when they witness the sometimes astonishing results of our meetings. In short, Beta isn't just good for the soul; it's also good for the bottom line.

Over the past five years, I've continually analyzed and refined my anthropological approach. As time goes on, and I help more and more companies adapt a successful Beta approach, I've become even more evangelical about the subject. My message may not be simple, but it offers extraordinary, and proven, opportunities.

In short:

Beta leaders and organizations enable people to succeed at what they're good at, rather than forcing them to become people they're not.

Beta leaders and organizations empower people to expand their skill sets based on individuals' own needs, rather than on a prescribed syllabus.

Beta leaders and organizations encourage people to confront and solve problems together, working collaboratively on the organization's shared mission.

Everyone in a Beta organization looks forward to coming to work. Employees' interests and the company's interests are aligned. The company doesn't just focus on the needs and interests of the top tier of executives, or an elite group of high-potential workers; it focuses on everybody. There is shared responsibility and a real, meaningful sense of community.

In a Beta organization, every employee—and not just those whose performance is in the top 10 percent—feels appreciated, as though they're participating fully in the company's mission, and getting their fair share of recognition and reward.

From a professional perspective, over the years I've discovered how to use and develop my own set of motivated skills: I've used cultural anthropology to build winning, high-impact corporate communities.

From a personal perspective, I've found my own small way to honor the inspiring community organizing of Annie Sullivan *and* my grandmother.

And from a business perspective, I've found a way to help companies position themselves to better lead and organize a successful twenty-first-century organization. The Beta approach and paradigm will help you recruit, manage, and retain the kind of talent you and your organization need to profit today and tomorrow. And the Beta mind-set will simultaneously provide you with a personal satisfaction you might have once brushed away as impossible.

We need to learn where we came from before we can learn where we're going next. As in all the important lessons shared around tribal fires, family hearths, and corporate conference tables, the story of Beta begins by looking backwards.

TWO

PLOWS AND PRIMATES

You have evolved from worm to man, but much within you is
still worm. Once you were apes, yet even now man is more
of an ape than any of the apes.

—FRIEDRICH NIETZSCHE, *Thus Spoke Zarathustra*

In the era when human societies were founded on hunting and
gathering, leadership was shared, fluid, and gender-equal. In winter, when there was little for the woman to gather, and the man was
able to track and bag a wild boar, he was the hero. But when summer came, and the male hunter arrived home with only a couple of
rodents for dinner, it must have been a hard sell to lord it over the
female gatherer who had provided a basketful of berries and another of hickory nuts.

The structure of prehistoric human societies was horizontal, not
hierarchical. There were still leaders, but they weren't autocrats.
Decisions were often made collaboratively by groups of elders, composed of both men and women. The voices of especially charismatic,
intelligent, experienced, or sage leaders may have carried a lot of
weight in these tribal councils, but the views and ideas of others
counted for a lot, too. The leader's voice didn't automatically win
out; he or she had to influence or convince others to agree.

The invention of the plow, which in turn led to the cultivation of crops, changed everything. Previously nomadic groups that had followed the migration of animal herds, or relocated to increase their chances of surviving the changing seasons, began to put down roots, both literally and figuratively. Agriculture required a time investment in a single setting. And staying in one place for an extended period of time gave people the opportunity to develop more permanent physical structures, villages, and societies. Hunting was still important, but over time its spoils became more a supplement than a staple of people's diets. A fixed location made the domestication of animals easier since people could now construct permanent enclosures. Rather than gathering wild flora, as they once had, societies began focusing on cultivating crops.

But instead of men shifting to animal husbandry and women shifting to crop cultivation, the male of the species began to dominate *both* aspects of food production. After all, early agriculture required an enormous amount of physical strength. Since males were and are inherently larger and stronger than women, they were better equipped to clear ground and break furrows with plows to plant seeds. As a result, men gained in status and importance over their female counterparts.

It didn't take very long for the strongest male to become the most revered member of the group. Gender roles began first to divide, and then to widen. In hunter-gatherer societies, both genders produced food and cared for children. But in agricultural societies, this changed: Men became the primary food producers, while women became the primary providers of child care. In the earliest human communities, this pattern of men working outside the home and women working inside the home took hold. Women might be called on to participate during the busiest planting and harvesting times, but they spent most of their time tending to their homes and offspring.

With strength now the most important survival trait, powerfully built young men became the elite. Elders and women who lacked male strength could only sit back and watch as the strength and value of their voices lost stature, too. Tribal councils, if they were still held, became formalities rather than occasions where groups came together to make decisions. And the most physically powerful members of the group began to assert their leadership over the others.

Before long, the horizontal structures of the preagricultural groups were replaced with hierarchical structures. Eventually, these informal hierarchies formalized into organizational pyramids, a form that would later become the organizing principle for practically all human groups, from clans to communities to countries to sports teams . . . to organizations and businesses. What's more, the command-and-control style of leadership replaced an approach I can best describe as communicate-and-collaborate.

(Perhaps the best-known example of this shift is the transformation of the Roman Republic by the Roman Empire under Augustus and his successors. Augustus made a great show of "consulting" the Senate, but the reality was that he was an absolute ruler: a toga-clad Alpha.)

The division of gender roles ended up creating a spiritual change across many societies as well. Before the development of agriculture, fertility was associated with females (for obvious reasons). Goddesses were worshipped in equal measure as gods; after all, without them, there would be no life. But as men began to assume dominant positions in society, and a more obvious role in the creation of new life—albeit plant life—male deities took center stage in the pantheons of gods, while cultures who worshipped a single deity presumed that higher power was male. The Great Father in the heavens replaced the Great Mother embodied by the earth, just as the male shaman replaced the wise woman. As a result, in many religions women were relegated to second-class clergy status, one they are still working to overcome today.

Those in power tend to use their own characteristics to establish a template for what defines a great leader. With men dominating the Agricultural Age, traits, skills, and approaches generally perceived as female—among them cooperation, collaboration, empathy, nurturing, communication, and compassion—were now viewed as secondary and subservient to those qualities perceived as male: strength, aggressiveness, command, dominance, and control. Women were labeled "the weaker vessel," and female attitudes, perspectives, and associated behaviors were weighed as less valuable and influential than what men brought to the equation. In short, anything other than the male approach was considered, at best, secondary.

Elizabeth I of England was a brilliant strategist and politician among other things, highly skilled at using her potential as a wife/ally and mother/dynast as diplomatic devices. She was accomplished at creating teams in her court made up of other powerful people, like Francis Walsingham, and Francis Drake. She also successfully led her nation through the difficult transition from Catholicism to Protestantism. But even Elizabeth I felt the need to adopt the mantle of the Alpha male when she found herself confronting the crisis of the Spanish Armada, in which a fleet of ships from that country sailed against England in an attempt to overthrow her monarchy. In 1588, the queen addressed her army, which had gathered at Tilbury to confront a potential invasion:

"I know I have the body but of a weak and feeble woman; but I have the heart and stomach of a king, and of a king of England too, and think foul scorn that Parma or Spain, or any prince of Europe, should dare to invade the borders of my realm; to which rather than any dishonour shall grow by me, I myself will take up arms, I myself will be your general, judge, and rewarder of every one of your virtues in the field."

With women busy carrying out the domestic responsibilities they were assigned in the agricultural age, men also became the primary practitioners of any newfound crafts that could bring in outside income. Men became masons, blacksmiths, brewers, coopers, farriers, millers, potters, weavers, and carpenters. It was men who entered the professional world, becoming doctors, lawyers, scientists, scholars, clergy, and politicians. Women weren't allowed to pursue any kind of apprenticeships or advanced education that would qualify them to become craftsmen or otherwise accredited members of society.

Nor was the dominance of this archetype, a powerful single leader with male character traits, limited to the home and the workplace.

For most of human history, autocrats—whether their titles were caesar, king, emperor, or first secretary—held military and political power. This model continued even as democracies began forming. Our founding fathers began their experiment with democracy by creating a loose collaborative form of government under the Articles of Confederation, in response to what they perceived as the extreme autocracy of George III. It was only after they experienced the occasional indecision and inactivity of poorly run collaborative efforts that they reached a compromise via the Constitution: presidents may be subject to the separation of powers, but they are still commanders in chief. Just as monotheistic religions established powerful earthly male leaders that mirrored the single omnipotent male leader in the sky, popes became infallible, while imams and rebbes remained the ultimate authorities in observant communities, as they still are today.

Not least, men rationalized the exclusion of females from these roles by suggesting they lacked the physical, mental, and even spiritual capabilities to handle these jobs and responsibilities. In retrospect, this movement—which eliminated opportunities for women and undoubtedly cost society the potential contributions of generations of females as everything from potters to physicians—seems absurd. Yet for many centuries it was accepted as fact. Even though women were the primary potters in Neolithic cultures, in subsequent centuries, none were given the chance to become Josiah Wedgwood. And it wasn't until 1849, after generations of midwives and nurses were excluded from the medical profession, that Elizabeth Blackwell graduated Geneva Medical School and became the first female physician in the United States. No one will ever know how many potential Marie Curies the world lost as a result.

Equally as damaging to society? That traits associated with women were perceived as incompatible with attaining success in agriculture, politics, religion, crafts, or for that matter, any worldly profession. The absence of a collaborative, nurturing spirit among political and religious leaders no doubt led to conflicts more often than not being settled by warfare. The complete lack of female anatomists probably meant medical advances arrived more gradually than they would have done otherwise. The absence of female voices in the halls of power may well have contributed to prolonged disputes between antagonistic nations. If we'd had just a few more female bankers in place sooner, for instance, it probably would not have taken centuries for microlending to become an established economic trend.

The Agricultural Revolution was responsible for the birth of the Alpha paradigm and the hierarchical organizational structure. But it was the next great technological revolution, the Industrial Revolution, that cemented the dominance of the strong, aggressive— that is to say, *male*—approach to leadership.

If the plow led to the Agricultural Revolution, the steam engine created the Industrial Revolution. Steam power replaced human power, making previously impossible tasks possible, and transforming individual production into mass production that, along with the assembly line, replaced small-scale agriculture, individual craftsmen, and small businesses. Assembly line work didn't demand the same kind of strength that plowing a field or shoeing a horse did. Nonetheless, assembly lines remained almost exclusively male domains. Physical strength mattered less than it ever had, but gender was now seen as the primary cause of women's second-class status. In the workplace, characteristics perceived and labeled as female continued to be denigrated. With all roads blocked to advancement, women become exclusively domestic workers. If they needed to work outside their own homes to provide additional income for their families, they did so in roles comparable to those they carried out inside their own homes: as cooks, maids, laundresses, or seamstresses.

In Industrial Age businesses, leadership was marked less by extreme physicality than by extreme competitiveness. Leaders no longer had to be *physically* stronger than everyone else; they had to be shrewder, more aggressive, and arguably, more relentless. Standard Oil founder John D. Rockefeller triumphed by destroying his rivals through means both fair and cunning. Even an innovative thinker like Thomas Edison made his name in part by beating down rivals like George Westinghouse and Nikola Tesla. It's no coincidence that the early titans of the Industrial Age were known as robber barons.

This take-no-prisoners leadership style not only compromised external relations between businesses, but it affected internal business life, too. There's only one spot atop the hierarchical pyramid, and countless generations fell into the trap of believing they needed to reach that pinnacle in order to achieve "success." When the sharp-elbowed narcissist made it to the top, he in turn became the archetype for how to succeed in business. Over time, people began to rationalize the crooked, ruthless, or manipulative behavior of industry captains or entrepreneurial "visionaries" as the baseline of what it took to succeed professionally.

As noted, as the Industrial Age got under way, the only professions open to women were those predicated on the nurturing of others, such as teacher and nurse. This typecasting was so extreme and widespread that its impact is still felt today. A quick glance at some recent statistics tells us that in 2012 more than 90 percent of nurses are female, while at the same time, women make up only 11 percent of engineers. Roughly 86 percent of elementary school teachers and more than 60 percent of secondary school teachers are female. Yet only 24 percent of full university professors and researchers are women. It's surely no coincidence that nursing and teaching remain among the two lowest-paid of all professions.

In desperate economic circumstances, society was willing to suspend these professional barriers, but only for the short term, that is, until the men came home. During the Great Depression, birthrates dropped and women who were the product of the socially liberated Roaring Twenties were encouraged to extend their freedom to economic spheres by bringing in as much outside income as they could. Might I add here that the boom and subsequent bust these women endured transformed them into an astonishingly resilient and independent generation?

A decade later, when World War II pulled millions of male workers from the workplace and put them in uniform, another generation of women was urged to swap its domestic roles for industrial work. Rosie the Riveter became an iconic symbol for the American woman's contributions on the home front. Not coincidentally, as women became a larger and increasingly vocal share of the population, the culture of many workplaces became less competitive and more relational. Organizations didn't become collaborative or horizontal overnight, but by becoming paternalistic rather than autocratic, they focused more on their employees' needs, including extending benefits for child care among female workers.

But when the war ended, and the GIs came home, women were

again pushed out of the workplace, child-care benefits vanished, and the macho workplace culture roared back to life stronger than ever. A more horizontal style of leadership might have worked on the home front, but a generation of men had spent the previous several years in the ultimate hierarchical organization, the U.S. military, where they grew accustomed to taking orders from their superiors and giving orders to those below them. Women were enjoined to view their fleeting economic independence as a temporary crisis measure. Now, once again, they were urged to devote themselves to being picture-perfect homemakers, tending to all those babies filling up those 1950s suburban tract houses, and ceding to men the workplace—a place that had become more top-down than ever before.

Society had to concoct new reasons to justify pushing Rosie the Riveter off the assembly line. After all, Rosie had helped forge the arsenal of democracy, an industrial colossus that won the war and split the atom. The forces that now insisted on a return to conventional gender roles could no longer claim that women were the weaker vessel, or that female skills and characteristics impeded accomplishment. They had to find new reasons. And in line with the nuclear and space preoccupations of the Cold War, traditionalists now began basing their pro-male, anti-female arguments on scientific case studies borrowed from the animal kingdom.

At the start of the twentieth century, North America and European scientists had begun studying animal behavior and group dynamics in depth. Among the earliest and most famous of these studies was one involving chickens. A Norwegian zoologist by the name of Thorleif Schjelderup-Ebbe spent much of his early life observing the behavior of barnyard fowl. In an academic paper published in 1921, he theorized that the social hierarchy among a group of chickens could be determined by the order in which they lined up to take their turn at the feed bowl. Schjelderup-Ebbe called this the *Hackordnung,* or the "pecking order."

At the same time, a handful of other European naturalists theorized that animal behaviors weren't endemic to a particular species, that they could be related to behaviors in other, unrelated species. Led by the Austrian biologists Konrad Lorenz and Karl von Frisch, these scientists dubbed this cross-species study of animal behaviors ethology. A similar idea was gaining traction in the United States, as psychologists were exploring animal behavior in the context of what they already knew—or thought they knew—about human behavior. Whether starting with the animals, as the Europeans did, or with human beings, as the Americans did, these two developing scientific fields came similarly to conclude that human and animal behavior were inextricably tied.

Now: If you're going to study the behavior of animals with the goal of applying your findings to humans, why not study human beings' closest animal relations, that is, primates? And rather than tracking down primates in the wild, and spending month after uncomfortable month in a gnat-filled bush, why not make it easy on yourself and pay a visit to the nearest zoo in order to observe captive gorillas and chimpanzees? For most of the twentieth century, this is precisely what scientists did. Their findings would later create the scientific justification for validating and extending both traditional gender roles and hierarchical leadership and organizations.

In short, scientists found that primate groups had no stable heterosexual relationships. Instead whether male or female, primates had any number of different mates. To no one's surprise, in most cases males were bigger and stronger than females. A clear hierarchy existed between the genders and within each gender. The strongest male could mate with as many and whichever females he chose. But while the dominant female retained her status all her life, the dominant male had to fight to reach the top, and keep fighting to maintain his authority. Very often these fights were political in nature, with the lower-status males joining forces in an attempt to displace the higher-status males. Yet in general, there was little serious violence in the group, which scientists theorized was based on primates understanding the unspoken rules of subservience and domination. In other words, everyone in the animal kingdom knew his or her place.

Australian zoologist Brian Gee described the dominant males as confident and physically intimidating. When necessary, they put on a display of strutting—shredding vegetation and charging to put the others in their place. Which, I have to admit, sounds a lot like some business executives I've known.

Ethologists and psychologists also observed that the early socializing of primates broke down along gender lines, too. Younger females spent most of their time with older females, and their play focused on the development of nurturing skills. In contrast, younger males spent their days play-fighting in groups made up entirely of other juvenile males.

By the late 1940s, scientists had begun to label the dominant male the Alpha male and the dominant female the Alpha female. They also theorized that the dominance patterns of our Darwinian ancestors were primitive but strikingly similar templates to the social structures among humans. From that day forward, the Alpha male metaphor was applied retroactively as well as forward. Success, past, present, and future, on the battlefield, the sporting field, in politics, in the bedroom, or in the boardroom, was entirely associated with Alpha male behavior. And just as younger primates were groomed to fit the mold, so were human children.

With its division of gender roles, its elevation and devaluation of traits dating back to the invention of the plow, the hierarchical style of leadership and organizational structure now had a formal name and an (evidently) scientific justification for being. To be successful in any and all fields, men and women both were advised to mimic the silverback gorilla pounding his chest and charging at rivals. They were advised to fight it out, to push, to strive. The nurturing, collaborative characteristics of female primates may have helped enable the group to survive, but they wouldn't get anyone even close to the top of the pack. At best they'd get you a pretty good but low-paying job as an elementary school teacher or a home health-care aide.

In the postwar years of the 1950s, Rosie the Riveter was replaced by June Cleaver. Pearls replaced red kerchiefs. Casseroles replaced biceps. The gender division between workplace and home was now even more pronounced, as was the corresponding division between what society encouraged in the workplace, versus at home. Men lived to work. Men traveled. Men barely saw their own children. Women did the opposite. Women devoted themselves to raising perfect (appearing) children and creating (outwardly) perfect homes. Girls were encouraged to play with dolls and toy kitchen appliances. They were enrolled in dance classes. Boys were expected to roughhouse and play with guns and bows and arrows. In contrast to the fox-trotting, waltzing girls, boys were enrolled in youth sports leagues. Even at public schools the girls filed obediently into home economics classes, while the boys busied themselves with woodworking and shop.

Women in the workforce weren't just constrained by their opportunities; they were also often physically segregated into discreet areas like secretarial pools. Many rightly observed that these subdivisions had a secondary function as a hunting ground for males to find sexual partners. For women, it sometimes seemed, the only route to success and power was through marriage to a successful, powerful man. But by marrying a 1950s Alpha male, and playing a role that was equal parts Betty Crocker, Mary Poppins, and Marilyn Monroe, many 1950s housewives found themselves defined exclusively by their relations to others: daughter, sister, wife, mother.

The Alpha paradigm had a profound impact on *all* our social interactions. The football team looked to the quarterback to lead the team. He was the one every little boy wanted to grow up to become, the one every middle-aged man covertly wished he could be. In clubs and organizations all across the country, groups selected or voted in presidents, convinced that without one, the members would fracture or collapse. In music, band members vied to become the group leader, the lead singer, the man with the mike. Even American families, most of which were patriarchies rather than genuine partnerships, weren't immune from the Alpha paradigm. "Wait 'til your father gets home from work" was a threat echoed in millions of American homes. The message couldn't be clearer: Mom was the nurturer, while Dad was the disciplinarian, the enforcer, the final word.

Society revered the lone wolf, the cowboy, the superhero. We celebrated and aspired to be the leader, the captain, the president, the CEO. We perceived leaders as decisive, risk-taking, and supremely confident—and if that meant they were also disagreeable, short-fused, or obnoxious, well, that was simply part of the equation. Alphas, after all, lived by different rules. They didn't have to "play well with others." Going it alone was seen as a positive. Better, after all, to risk everything and go for broke than to settle for the compromise of coming in second or third. Did any Olympic athlete *really* set out to win a bronze medal?

The good news is that elsewhere, change was beginning to foment. The seeds of two new revolutions, one social and the other technological, had begun to flower. Moreover, new research was calling into question traditional scientific rationalizations for the existence and lionization of the Alpha male. All of which would come together to herald the birth of a new, healthier, and in all ways far superior approach: Beta.

THREE

BOOMERS AND BONOBOS

Each suburban wife struggled with it alone. As she made the beds,
shopped for groceries . . . she was afraid to ask even of herself
the silent question—"Is this all?"

—BETTY FRIEDAN, *The Feminine Mystique*

For centuries, the hierarchical style and structure that I call the Alpha paradigm was the only way leaders led, and the only way organizations organized. Leaders asserted themselves aggressively, competed rather than collaborated, and conquered rather than compromised, which trickled down to younger generations as the single template of how to be, act, behave, and aspire. Organizations were constructed like pyramids, with predetermined and narrowly defined steps or rungs leading to the top. The slightest suggestion of a more community-oriented or compassionate approach was seen as "soft," certainly not sufficient to lead a "tough" organization through "tough" times. Not least, flatter, more horizontal structures were seen as inefficient, undeservedly egalitarian, and perhaps even un-American.

Yet World War II mandated that societies adopt an altogether different approach. With large numbers of men in the military, societies had to unbuckle gender barriers and push women to assume workplace roles traditionally held by men. That, and the need for labor and management to come together to fight a common enemy, led to a markedly less aggressive, more paternalistic style of leadership. With far fewer ambitious men crowding the corporate ranks, there was far less politicking. Many companies became more horizontal. Interestingly, the victorious Allied countries—the United States, the United Kingdom, and the Soviet Union—were most responsible for lowering gender barriers, in contrast to Germany and Japan. Fascists were irredeemable Alphas; a phenomenon that doubtlessly contributed to their ultimate defeat.

When the war ended, and the men came home, gender barriers and organizational pyramids swiftly reasserted themselves. In an effort to restore prewar values, and apply newfound military attitudes and behaviors to the workplace that a generation of American men had just acquired abroad, gender barriers became more entrenched, just as the reconstructed organizational pyramids became even steeper. Leaders became militaristic rather than paternalistic, though perhaps the aggressive reassertion of the traditional Alpha paradigm was born of a fear that the genie may have slipped out of the bottle? After all, once society removes the shackles of individual freedom, it's practically impossible to go backwards.

In 1957, Betty Friedan, a journalist who lost her job when she became pregnant with her second child, decided to conduct a survey of her classmates from the Smith College class of 1942. An overwhelming number of full-time homemakers reported back that they felt trapped and unhappy with their lives. In *The Feminine Mystique,* the book her research inspired, Friedan memorably dubbed her classmates' malaise "the problem that has no name." With its message that women were as capable as men of following any and all career paths, but were imprisoned by the narrow roles society asked them to follow, *The Feminine Mystique* became a national phenomenon. Today, Friedan's book is commonly cited by critics and social scientists as the kindling that ignited the rebirth of the Women's Movement.

It wasn't only women who responded so strongly to Friedan's book. Many men realized their lives lacked meaning, too. Published in 1954, Sloan Wilson's *The Man in the Gray Flannel Suit* was a national bestseller that caused many men to take a hard look at their own spiritual emptiness. Exploring the struggle to find happiness in a time of conformity and materialism, Wilson's novel struck a deep chord in many discontented wannabe Alpha males. The disconnect between the image and the reality of what being an Alpha really means still resonates today. Viewers tune in to watch the hit show *Mad Men* not just to admire the stylish performances of Jon Hamm and January Jones, but to follow the emotional and psychological volatility of Don and Betty Draper as they navigate the 1950s and 1960s.

That era, I might add, should have been a Golden Age for Americans. The United States was the world's acknowledged superpower. Honed to perfection during the war, our industrial economy had created an affluent consumer society that the rest of the world envied. Everything was growing: the economy, the tail fins of cars, the boundaries of urban areas, the width of movie screens, even the size of families. Yet Friedan and Wilson had both uncovered a hidden truth: that beneath the veneer of confident affluence was a gaping lack of emotional and psychological fulfillment.

The children of these frustrated 1950s families were reared to desire and expect the most out of life. They were both empowered and entitled. The sheer size of their generation impelled society to accommodate their needs, whether by building more schools or by giving them sway over the nation's culture. Their fathers and mothers had made the world safe for democracy, but these young people planned on evolving that same world to the next level. Heady with confidence, many set out to find the self-fulfillment lacking in their own parents, which they expressed in a countercultural movement that encompassed everything from foreign policy and civil rights to music and the workplace.

Work began to be seen not just as a way to earn a decent living, but as a way to make a lasting difference. Overnight, the concept of "meaningful work" began to take hold. William H. Whyte, an editor at *Fortune* magazine, stared down the Alpha-driven business world of the Industrial Age and, like Friedan and Wilson before him, wasn't entirely happy with what he saw. In his 1956 book, *The Organization Man*, Whyte provided a mainstream sociological critique of the workplace in many ways similar to the counterculture's own argument. America, he observed, was creating a hierarchical society that discouraged individual initiative and expression by demanding that everyone squeeze him- or herself into rigidly defined patterns and roles.

Young men of the 1960s and 1970s sauntered into the workplace with the intention of liberalizing it. They would replace the buttoned-down collars of their fathers with cool turtlenecks. As society sought to create jobs for this incoming workforce, the ranks of middle management swelled. As representatives of the largest group of affluent potential customers the world had ever seen, these young executives climbed the corporate ladder more quickly than their fathers ever could have dreamed of doing. Competition was stiff for what was then still only a small number of upper-level positions. Political skills honed by organizing student protests now found their place around conference tables. The entitlement bred into many of these young men as children blossomed into grown-up materialism. Wannabe hippies who craved VWs grew up to become yuppies who lusted for BMWs. Sure, unlike their fathers, they had avoided becoming Organization Men, but as they took their positions in the C Suite, by now they resembled characters in Tom Wolfe's *Bonfire of the Vanities*. Instead of revolutionaries devoted to making the world a better place, they now plotted to become Masters of the Universe.

What about their female counterparts? Embracing the label of "feminist," young women of the 1960s and 1970s did everything they could to bust out of their assigned roles as homemakers and demolish workplace gender barriers. Striving for equal pay for equal work, they streamed into the job force in large numbers. Unfortunately, their male counterparts weren't exactly eager to give up their workplace hegemony. These men had grown up with stay-at-home moms who greeted them at the door after school, and cleaned up after their messes . . . and they naturally assumed their girlfriends and wives would do the same. A bitter joke of the time was that when the members of an ostensibly egalitarian hippie collective gathered, the men still expected the women to bake the brownies and tidy up after the meeting. Sadly, what was true for the collective was even more so in the workplace.

Many women battled back against sexism and broke through the glass ceiling. The problem was, to do so they had to adopt the attitudes, behaviors, and even the wardrobes of men and sacrifice their more humane, nurturing selves; they had to become Alpha females. Soon the stereotype of the cold, calculating career woman entered the culture. It soon became a tired trope, whether it was Diane Keaton playing an executive nicknamed the Tiger Lady who becomes complete only when she "inherits" a child in *Baby Boom*, or Demi Moore playing a sexually rapacious Alpha female in *Disclosure*. Instead of women humanizing the workplace, the workplace threatened to dehumanize women. That said, these women did manage to leave a lasting impact—as role models to their own sons and daughters.

Which brings us to today.

Instead of being raised in families that resembled the Cleavers of *Leave It to Beaver*, today's knowledge workers were reared in households that more closely resembled the Huxtables of *The Cosby Show*. Many came from homes where gender roles were fluid, constantly at play, and where few families believed that women were any less capable than men. Not all of their parents would be comfortable labeling themselves as feminists, but it's safe to say that almost all believed their daughters and sons could become whoever and whatever they wanted. In elementary schools, boys and girls were no longer divided into two separate lines, with the boys funneled into shop classes and the girls streaming into home economics. Today's knowledge workers grew up in a cultural and professional environment where women were physicians, pilots, business executives, and soldiers. Many of these women may have been forced to adopt male behavior patterns and attitudes to succeed, but in the end, they showed the world that women could compete with men in every conceivable field and do very nicely, thank you.

Female success, then, was a given to many of these young children. In sports, many competed against both boys and girls on equal terms. They grew up with the topic of homosexuality not merely out of the closet, but on prime-time television. To most, traditional notions of manliness and femininity came across as archaic, even ironical. They thought nothing about a man sporting an earring or a woman with a buzz cut. Gender-specific home economics and shop classes evolved into mixed consumerism and technology classes. A majority of today's knowledge workers were raised in community-oriented environments that emphasized teamwork and group successes. There wasn't a single "top dog": every player on the team got a trophy. The upshot? A generation that doesn't perceive character traits as either "male" or "female," or make the mistake of believing that success is an individual achievement.

It's also a generation marked by female achievement. In 2005, for example, statistics showed that for the first time ever, women under thirty living in major American cities had overtaken their same-aged male counterparts in earning power. As consumer behaviorist Paco Underhill writes, "This increase in female earning power parallels employment figures around the globe. Starting in the United States, with its then-current 2009 employment rate of 8.5 percent, the chances of being twenty-five years old and gain-fully employed are higher if you're a female than if you're a male."[1] He adds, "Economic hard times favor females, too. During the re-cent recession, 82 percent of job losses befell men, who tend to be disproportionately represented in industries like construction and manufacturing. Historically, women are apt to work in fields like education and health care, which are more resistant to economic swings."[2]

Thanks also to birth control and the ability to choose when and if they have children, women are today making notable profes-sional strides. They dominate higher education. They are attending business schools in historic numbers. Industries like the military and farming that have traditionally called upon muscle no longer require brawn, but instead demand qualities like focus, diligence, and an eye for detail. "Almost 40 percent of U.S. working wives now outearn their husbands, a percentage that has risen steeply in this country and many others, as more women have entered the workforce and remained committed to it," writes author Liza Mundy in her book *The Richer Sex.* "Women occupy 51 percent of managerial and professional jobs in the United States, and they dominate nine of the ten U.S. job categories expected to grow the most in the next decade."[3] Pay inequalities between the sexes are still prevalent—a dozen years after graduation, female Harvard alumni earn 30 percent less than their male classmates—but for women, the Information Age has made the world flatter than it's ever been before.

Nor do most of today's Information Age workers believe that they have to become Alpha males in order to succeed in the world. What better example is there than NBA star LeBron James? Widely considered the greatest basketball player in the world, James par-layed his free agent status into becoming one of a ferociously skilled threesome. Older athletes criticized his move to the Miami Heat where he joined fellow superstars Dwyane Wade and Chris Bosh, suggesting James should join a team where he could be top dog, proving he could single-handedly win his team the championship. All I can say is that when a professional athlete of LeBron James's caliber turns his back on the Alpha paradigm, you know times are changing.

As were the scientific attitudes that served to rationalize the reinstatment of the Alpha paradigm in the years after World War II. It was now clear to everyone that women could succeed beyond anyone's expectations at doing "men's work," and that a horizontal leadership style was just as effective as, if not even more effective than, the previous paradigm.

In recent years, new generations of ethologists and comparative psychologists have also reconsidered the findings of their predecessors. New theories have pulled away the fragile scientific veneer that protected the Alpha paradigm.

Today, scientists realize that both male and female behavior is profoundly influenced by environment, and is often the consequence of socialized learning. They have also criticized the idea that a field researcher could elicit valid data from observing animals, whether primates in a zoo or chickens in a coop. When scientists carried out their first primate studies, zoos squeezed as many animals as they could into cramped enclosures that provided limited resources for the animals' health and well-being. In nine cases out of ten, the inevitable result was a stressful, highly unnatural environment. Is it any wonder those animals were so aggressive and competitive?

Even as zoos modernized and updated, they were still in the business of creating artificial environments where animals couldn't hunt, mating was choreographed, and caretakers provided food. Coming up with theories on primate behavior based on observations of animals in captivity is the equivalent of coming up with theories about human behavior based on observations of prisoners on death row.

Scientists are even calling into question the earliest primate studies on natural free-ranging populations that their peers carried out in the wild. Anthropologist and primatologist Sarah Blaffer Hrdy went so far as to theorize that the traditional concept of the Alpha male is nothing less than a crude form of projection by male scientists. The idea that there's a single top male who gets to mate with all the females and dominate the other males, she speculated, had more to do with the fantasy lives of all those early evolutionary biologists, many of whom were elite males themselves.

Maybe that's one reason why renowned anthropologist Louis Leakey preferred to sponsor female observers of great apes in the wild. He handpicked Jane Goodall to study chimpanzees, Diane Fossey to study gorillas, and Birutė Galdikas to study orangutans. Their contemporary studies of primates in the natural habitats have led to a less sexist assessment of the roles played by males and females. Many of the most interesting studies came about from observing the behavior of bonobos who, like chimpanzees, share 99 percent of the same DNA as human beings. (At the time of Leakey's death in 1972, he was in the process of arranging for a fourth woman, Toni Jackman, to launch a project observing bonobos.)

The dynamics of bonobo society shattered the myth of the Alpha male as an innate primate characteristic, and therefore a natural paradigm for human society. Even though male bonobos are generally larger and stronger than the females, bonobo groups are matriarchies. Scientists have observed few aggressive encounters between male and female bonobos, and when it happens, the females band together to discourage excessively aggressive behavior by the individual males.

Bonobos use sex to create bonds, and to reduce stress and aggressiveness. Female bonobos use their sexuality to control male members of the pack. Whereas chimpanzees commonly attack males from neighboring packs who wander into their territory, bonobos initiate sexual contact with scouts from other packs. Both male and female bonobos have been observed engaging in homosexual behavior as a bonding activity.

As for the status of males in a bonobo group, it's determined not by strength or aggressiveness, but by the status of their mothers. The bond between mothers and sons remains strong and enduring throughout the animals' lives. Frans de Waal, the Dutch primatologist and ethologist, characterizes bonobos as altruistic, compassionate, empathetic, and patient. Contemporary ethologists suggest that if you don't have to be an aggressive, physically intimidating, chest-pounding Alpha male to lead a pack of bonobos, then just maybe you don't need to be one to lead a pack of people, either.

If observations of bonobo behavior weren't enough to throw the entire scientific basis for the Alpha paradigm into question, genetic research has also caused us to reexamine the notion of assigned gender roles and traits.

Gender, it seems, isn't the straightforward issue many scientists had always assumed. Some species can't even be categorized as being either "male" or "female"; they may begin life as one sex and mutate in response to an environmental variation. In some cases they may go so far as to function as both male *and* female. In its larval stage, *Bonellia,* a green sea worm, becomes either male or female based on where it lands on the seabed. If it lands a distance from any other sea worms, it becomes female. If it floats down beside a female, it becomes male. While admittedly human beings are a lot more developed than green sea worms, even our own gender identity isn't so starkly defined as most of us believe.

Today we know that every human being begins life with the potential to develop as either male or female—and that sex is determined by whether the single sperm cell that fertilizes an egg contributes an X or Y chromosome. Since every sperm carries equal numbers of X and Y chromosomes, gender determination at the point of fertilization is spectacularly random. In his book, *The X in Sex,* reproductive biologist David Bainbridge writes, "The acquisition of our most important trait has turned out to resemble the tossing of a coin." As we develop, gender doesn't get much more definitive than that: scientists believe that even this chromosomal pattern isn't perfectly predictive of gender.

After a number of female athletes from the Communist Bloc had their gender called into question during the Cold War, women competing in the Olympic Games were required to undergo sex testing. The test was designed to detect the presence of the Y chromosome, which is present in males but not in females. If an athlete was found to have a Y chromosome, she was ineligible to compete as a female. But as science uncovered more information about chromosomes and gender, it became obvious that the test was inadequate.

Even though the XX chromosomal pattern typically results in a female, and the XY in a male, approximately one of every 20,000 women is actually born with the XY pattern—a condition known as "androgen insensitivity." This means simply that their bodies do not respond to the genetic information contained in their Y chromosome. Unless women undergo testing, they may live through their lives without realizing they are biologically male. Which, among other things, means that since the invention of the plow, the .005 percent of females who were told they couldn't do a man's job were, in fact, biologically men.

Due in no small part to privacy and discrimination issues (after all, men are seldom if ever tested to confirm their maleness), the International Olympic Committee abandoned sex testing in 1999. A handful of sports federations still use sex testing in specific cases, but these assessments usually combine chromosomal assessment with examinations by gynocologists, endocrinologists, internists, and psychologists. Following science's lead, society is gradually accepting that gender and sexuality are far more fluid, porous, and complex than we ever knew.

As definitions of gender come into question, so does the way we perceive traits and behaviors traditionally characterized as either "male" or "female." Biologists have discovered that empathy and other social skills typically viewed as "female" actually originate in males, and are passed along from fathers. Studies have also shown that individuals with lower levels of testosterone are better equipped to handle stressful situations. Contrary to centuries of faulty assumptions, this means that women are less likely to break under pressure than their male counterparts.

Social science research also conclusively shows that women can be just as effective as leaders and investors as men. For example, in Indian villages, where locals laws mandate female leadership in at least one-third of the nation's village councils, research conducted by economist Esther Duflo shows female leadership to be objectively superior: Women leaders constructed a higher number of new wells, were better at maintaining existing wells, and accepted fewer bribes from village officials. What's more, through his Grameen Bank, Nobel Prize–winning economist Muhammad Yunus offers 97 percent of his microloans to women. Why? Women, it turns out, use this money far more effectively than men.

These recent findings don't mean men are better than women at social skills, or that women are better than men at leading and investing. We can merely conclude that the traits and skills necessary to succeed cannot be defined or quantified by sex. Attempting to quantify male versus female brains, a recent Cambridge University study apologetically noted that a fifth of male study subjects appeared to have female-wired brains, while a fifth of the women they studied seemed to have male-wired brains.

If being male no longer means you have to be competitive, risk-taking, and willing to go it alone, then maybe it's okay for a male business leader to serve not as an omniscient, omnipotent autocrat, but as a collaborative team player.

Social changes that have taken place since the 1960s created a widespread demand for a new way to organize ourselves and lead our organizations, while scientific advances were busy overturning long-standing rationalizations for the old Alpha paradigm. The only thing left that we needed to help launch a brand-new paradigm? A full-fledged technological revolution.

FOUR

INFORMATION CHANGES EVERYTHING

The change from atoms to bits is irrevocable and unstoppable. Why now? Because the change is also exponential—small differences of yesterday can have suddenly shocking consequences tomorrow.

—NICHOLAS NEGROPONTE, *Being Digital*

Information technology has transformed just about everything. I'm hardly alone in believing that the combination of the digital computer and wireless communications will have as widespread, dramatic, and long-lasting an impact on human society as the invention of the plow did in the eighteenth and nineteenth centuries. And just as the plow led to the development of the Alpha paradigm for organizing groups of people, so information technology today sets the stage for the wholly new organizing system that I call Beta.

In the years leading up to today's Information Age, the essential structure of organizations and institutions was the pyramid. This structure was reflected not just in the business as a whole, but across separate parts of the organization. Divisions within the company, departments within the divisions, and teams within those departments all followed this same pattern.

The pyramid matched the very nature of work itself. In the Industrial Age, both blue- and white-collar work was largely algorithmic: it consisted of rote, repetitive tasks that adhered to a formula or pattern. This in turn demanded a large number of "assembly line" workers, whether they were building cars, compiling animated films, or filling in tax returns. These were the people at the very bottom of the pyramid. With the front-line staff busy assembling, there had to be a cadre of people who supervised their efforts and collected data on their results. This group made up the next level of the pyramid: managers. Next, the work of these bottom two levels had to be studied and put into context so that businesses could make sound judgments. That was the task of the third level: analysts. The reports prepared by the analysts ended up on the desks of a fourth level of employees tasked with ensuring the efforts of the lower three levels were leading the branches of the organization in desired directions: executives. Setting those directions was the next level: strategists, who charted the course for an element or division of the company. Finally, atop the strategists was the leader, the individual who set forth the overall mission of the organization as a whole. This structure fit and complemented the Alpha paradigm. Each level of the organization reported to its own Alpha, while ascending the chart to the ultimate Alpha: the CEO.

This structure, which probably originated with feudalism and was later popularized by the military, led to a "silo effect." Meaning, little or no cooperation existed among the various teams within a department, departments with a division, or divisions within a company. Why? Because peers at every level felt as though they were competing directly for only a handful of available promotions. This competition was exacerbated by typical budgeting policies and procedures that allocated funds based on prior performance and politics, rather than on current and future organizational needs. As a result, people at every level underpromised, then overdelivered, in order to get a bigger slice of the budget pie than their "competitors."

The end result? Individuals often focused more on their perceived internal competitors than on their actual external competitors. Strategists typically spent more time and energy worrying about where and how they stacked up against the company's other strategists than where the company stood in relation to other companies in the same market. As long as this kind of internal competition worked, it was tolerated, and in some instances even encouraged. In the 1920s, Alfred Sloan, CEO of General Motors, deliberately created divisions within his own company, obliging company brands like Chevy and Pontiac to compete for the same prototypical car buyer. In the 1930s, Procter & Gamble took a similar approach, assigning various brands to groups of employees who then had to fight not just for market share but for resources against other P&G brands as well.

The silos created by the organizational pyramid could also prevent information from being shared. One team might have no idea what another team across the room was doing. Groups might very well be duplicating each other's efforts, maybe even working at cross purposes. One division might not share its customer list with another division, just as one department whose expertise was in one field might be reluctant to pass along that expertise to another department whose client needed help, opting instead to pursue its own proprietary relationship with that client.

With information so closely held, and with rivalrous Alphas at every level and corner of the organization, decision-making in the Industrial Age belonged to only a small group of people. Input might be solicited from customers, or from the rank and file, but typically this was little more than a public relations exercise on the part of the organization. Whether they were on the front lines or even in senior management, employees excluded from the inner circle believed they needed to keep their mouths shut if they ever wanted to get ahead. They had good reason, too. After all, they had seen non-core-group colleagues speak their minds, and afterwards find themselves at best ignored, at worst terminated. As a result, few said anything. This often worked to the detriment of the organization, since it failed to welcome new ideas or heed prescient warnings.

The best example of ignoring employee input is the so-called Promethean Myth of the Information Age. In 1979, Xerox executives invited Steve Jobs and a team of engineers from Apple Computer to visit the copier giant's Palo Alto Research Center, known as PARC. The Xerox engineers working on the operational side of business at PARC knew this invitation was a mistake. They knew Xerox had the keys to the future kingdom in its hands, and didn't want them handed over to the people from Apple. The operational Betas bravely spoke up. But the Alpha executives, evidently having been promised shares in the upcoming Apple stock offering, brushed aside what they said. Reluctantly, Xerox engineers showed their guests laser printing, the mouse, the windows, the folders, the ethernet networking, and the pull-down menus. You probably know what happened next. Apple became the champion of the graphical user interface, which revolutionized computing and launched the Information Age, and Xerox lost its chance to become a dominant player in a technology that would define the future. As for those PARC engineers whose voices were ignored? I'm happy to report that most left Xerox to become founders or major players in major Information Age companies.

The Industrial Age organization placed a premium on seniority. Algorithmic work didn't demand much creativity or innovation. Changes were, at most, incremental, while problems and opportunities remained the same year after year. What mattered most for this type of work was the wisdom born of experience. The longer employees spent at any one level, the better they were qualified for the next level. As a result, employers based most promotions on an employee's length of service. If staffers had to be cut, the default rule was "last hired, first fired."

In the Industrial Age, most business was local or regional. Although there were national and international transportation and communication available, it was expensive and time-consuming. What's more, markets tended to be unique and self-contained. Products popular in the Southeast, for example, were essentially unknown in the Northwest. Even companies that had a national or international presence tended to refine and tailor their offerings in behalf of regional preferences. Kraft Foods might have one brand of cookies tailored for Northeastern tastes, and another carefully designed for midwestern tastes.

But information technology turned this model around. As I mentioned earlier, nowadays most work is experience-based, intuitive, and commonsensical rather than algorithmic. Digital computers and their accompanying technology have mechanized the rote work of the past. Today, robots are assembling cars. Software is filling out tax returns. Bar codes can collect data electronically. In the Information Age, both blue- and white-collar work seldom involves routine patterns, but instead requires creative problem-solving.

The ability to digitize and store data and to automate processes and procedures makes experience a lot less valuable. A database and a sophisticated application can replace a decade's worth of working a particular job. Similarly, the ability to collect and compare enormous amounts and varieties of data makes analysis easier and acquired insight less essential. As a result, older, higher-paid individuals are being replaced by younger, lower-paid coworkers. The ability to create, acquire, manipulate, and interpret digitized information has taken precedence over any wisdom that might be acquired via hands-on experience.

The already-legendary connectivity afforded by information technology has created an environment where individuals are able to provide their own ideas and feelings about everything from national politics to the relative merits of toaster ovens. This ability to provide input has in turn created additional demands to, well, provide input. People today want and expect the freedom to comment about everything from family photos to their company's strategy. Company intranet sites and wikis generate as much activity as national sports teams' message boards.

Similarly, the ubiquity of information today has created additional demands for information among both employees and customers. For generations, Alpha executives kept the tightest possible grip on communication. They were paranoid about leaks. They believed that, like children, employees didn't need to know any more than was necessary to carry out their day-to-day responsibilities. In the Information Age, this approach has been turned upside down. "The sense of entitlement senior executives had around information is vanishing," says Fred Wilson, a leading venture capitalist and principal of his own New York–based firm, Union Square Ventures. "In most of our successful companies, the CEOs are having weekly meetings and being fairly open and honest with the rank and file about what is going on. Tech companies know that for the rank and file to feel loyal to the company, to buy into it, they need to feel they're being kept in the loop."

All of this communication capability and activity is more than just a public relations and morale-boosting effort. In many organizations, it has been turned into practical decision-making and production methodologies.

Open source is a methodology in which the origins, methods, and plans underlying a finished product are made available at no cost, so that everyone can contribute to the improvement and adaptation of the product. The creation of the Internet itself was an open source project, one in which telecommunications protocols were developed through public requests for comments. Today, open source is best known as the driving force behind software like the Linux Operating System, the Apache Web server, Mozilla Firefox Web browser and Mozilla Thunderbird e-mail client, and the OpenOffice.org office software suite.

Crowd sourcing is another practical methodology that originated from the connectivity and community created by information technology. Typically, crowd sourcing involves a problem that is then presented to a large network or community in a request for solutions, which the community then rates. Contributors aren't always compensated materially; sometimes they receive simple recognition, while other times they contribute for no reason other than personal satisfaction. This system allows problems to be explored quickly and at low cost, often by a much broader range of talent than an organization could otherwise draw on. In addition, by using crowd sourcing, the sponsoring organization receives intelligence on the feelings and motivations of its constituents, which can promote a real sense of shared ownership.

As Daniel Pink writes in his book *Drive,* two decades ago few people would have predicted that Wikipedia, an encyclopedia compiled and perennially updated by unpaid volunteers, would force Encarta, an authoritative encyclopedia backed with the resources of Microsoft (then the most powerful computer company in the world) out of business. Today, *Group Think* is no longer a fear-mongering term. Group Think is actually being harnessed to address everything from the search for intelligent life in the universe to seeking a cure for cancer.

Whether or not an organization actively uses methods such as open source and crowd sourcing in its operations, in the Information Age it is vital that a company's constituents feel that their voices are being heard. This requires a different approach from that of Alpha. It doesn't mean that all companies should wake up tomorrow as democracies, or strive to make all decisions based on consensus. It means simply that today's workers need an opportunity to present their opinions and ideas.

When coupled with advances in communications and transportation, information technology has also served to break down barriers of distance. Documents that once had to be mailed or physically transported by messengers are today sent as e-mail attachments. Thanks to the Internet, cottage businesses can now address a global audience, allowing them to give up the cottage along the way and become entirely virtual. Immigrants who used to phone home to the mother country once a year now trade daily e-mails or Skype with relatives thousands of miles away. Products can be designed in Boston, have parts built in Switzerland, be assembled in Colorado, then marketed and sold out of Austin, Texas.

Contributing to the intersection of technology and globalization is the breakdown of economic and political barriers. The collapse of communism everywhere except for Cuba Laos, Vietnam, China, and North Korea has created a world open to capitalist commerce. My guess? It's only a matter of time before these last two holdouts join the crowd. Trade barriers are crumbling by design or default, through the creation of multinational units like the European Union; trade pacts such as NAFTA; or the simple human desire to trade. Cultural differences remain, but there's an almost universal drive to overcome them with the shared goal of making money.

Again, capability has engendered demand. The possibility of doing business globally has inevitably led to the requirement of being global in order to compete. Manufacturing and customer service today not only *can* be outsourced, but typically *must* be outsourced. And since most companies and organizations aren't large or affluent enough to launch overseas arms, partnerships and joint ventures have become commonplace, which has further broken down geographic, cultural, and political barriers while simultaneously empowering the masses. In a world where everyone across the globe can potentially access identical information, connectivity becomes a source of nearly unparalleled power.

Just as important as the opportunities that globalization presents is the change it requires in attitude and approach. Throughout the Industrial Age, many businesses aspired to become self-contained, all-powerful Alpha organizations. Most leadership teams believed they needed complete control over every aspect of their businesses. Some even created the company town, where everything from the raw materials of manufacturing to the homes where employees lived was company-owned. The globalization of the Information Age compels all businesses, whether autocratic or philanthropic, to accept that they cannot do everything, everywhere, on their own. Naturally, interconnectivity comes with a cost. When Iceland's economy sneezed, all of Europe caught a cold. And when India tightens its sari, the squeeze is felt from Africa to the Arab Emirates.

Globalization has affected more than just business. It has also infiltrated popular culture. Individuals who three decades earlier might have remained minor figures, like English singer Susan Boyle, are today international celebrities. Professional soccer, a global mania in most countries outside the United States, today finds itself competing for fans on its own turf with European basketball and American baseball and football. Food trends both high- and low-end today spread with the speed of text messages. An innovative chef from Beirut can soon find her signature cooking style replicated in a Las Vegas restaurant. And a consumer can find a McDonald's anywhere from Hungary to China to Italy, as well as across Latin America.

No matter how charismatic or visionary they are, aggressive, domineering Alpha leaders find themselves swimming against the currents of the Information Age. Dictators who have withstood generations of protest and anger are being brought down by young people who use Facebook, Google, Tumblr, and Twitter to organize and convey their messages to the rest of the world. These same young people employ other technologies, including cellular networks, to dodge governmental efforts to "shut down" the Internet. The fax machine was the primary weapon protestors used in Peking's Tiananmen Square back in 1989, until it proved unable to stand up to tanks. Twenty-two years later, protestors in Cairo's Tahrir Square found Twitter worked better.

Old boys' networks in business are also crumbling under the power and ubiquity of LinkedIn networks. Whether they're corporate bullies or government dictators, authoritarian leaders are no longer immune to the comments and criticisms of large numbers of people with access to information. Anyone can become an influential player in almost any field through the power of their ideas spread virally as a blog entry or a video posted on YouTube. Just as disappointed customers can post negative product reviews and affect national sales, so angry employees can post comments on a blog about what they perceive to be a faulty strategy, and that way, send a message to the entire company.

By now I hope it's clear that the Information Age demands a new approach to organizing groups of people, as well as to functioning *within* those same organizations. The Alpha paradigm no longer fits today's world. We need a new approach to business that doesn't rely on seniority and other strict traditional patterns of advancement and growth; an approach that gives employees and customers the ability and opportunity to acquire information and express themselves; and not least, an approach that promotes greater teamwork, both internally and externally. Did anyone say Beta?

FIVE

COMMUNICATION, COLLABORATION, AND CURATION

Individual commitment to a group effort—that is what makes a team work, a company work, a society work, a civilization work.

—VINCE LOMBARDI

To flourish in today's business environment, organizations and individuals need to swap the outdated Alpha system for the fast-growing Beta paradigm.

Again, what is Beta? Beta is the communitarian, horizontal alternative to the individualistic, hierarchical Alpha paradigm. Beta creates networks rather than silos. Beta deemphasizes secrecy, and focuses instead on the pooling of information, ideas, and opinions. Beta emphasizes teamwork over individual competition. Beta is a paradigm that lets people play to their strengths and pursue paths that offer personal satisfaction, instead of labeling them and channeling them into predetermined categories and patterns. Beta is marked by shared leadership responsibility. And at its core, Beta is about three things: communication, collaboration, and curation.

Historically, executives in traditional Alpha organizations hoarded communication, treating it like an extraordinarily rare commodity; an instrument worth tucking away, to be used later on for individual benefit.

A new, entry-level employee of an Alpha organization might find that a veteran colleague keeps knowledge about how to do certain tasks to himself, hoping to keep the newcomer from becoming a potential threat to his own authority and position. Wary of losing leverage, Alpha managers may conceal deadlines and budgets from other staffers. Departments can withhold information from other departments in Alpha organizations, in an effort to maintain power and influence. And Alpha executives may refrain from sharing strategic goals and corporate developments with staff, fearing disclosure or actions that might undermine future plans or initiatives. The culture of most Alpha organizations? Give people information solely on a need-to-know basis. Everything else is if not top secret, then for executives' eyes only.

Now, most Industrial Age workers didn't expect to know what others in the company did. They were simply encouraged to do their job and keep their heads down. Bosses seldom sought out unsolicited ideas and opinions; in fact, to this day, many supervisors treat "suggestions" as veiled criticisms. The most virulently secretive Alpha companies are said to practice what some have dubbed "mushroom management": They keep their employees in the dark, cover them with dung, and when they get big enough, can them.

In a world where increasing numbers of businesses court the press by encouraging their employees to blog or tweet, Apple is notoriously secretive, to the point of spreading disinformation about product development among its own people. Security doors, security cameras, prototypes shrouded in black cloaks, and a legacy of hunting down suspected leakers and threatening legal action against bloggers who violate what the company calls "trade secret" laws are just a few examples of Apple's locked-down environment.[1]

To be fair to Apple, secrecy is the norm in many large companies. But there *are* no secrets anymore (and if there are, rest assured that someone, somewhere, will uncover them). Today, *conversa-*

tional media rules the day. Whether they know it or not, all companies and brands are in the business of engaging with consumers and addressing their concerns, complaints, and compliments. Business today is an ongoing dialogue—a lifelong conversation. In an environment where consumers have an unmatched amount of power, corporate transparency is essential.

Think about it: Customers have gadgets—iPhones, iPads, Black-Berries, Androids—and they're fearless about using them. Thanks to Twitter, Facebook, Yelp, and countless other companies and Web sites, today just about everyone has a dais, a microphone, an opinion, a high-resolution camera and video-player, and the means to upload or convey that insight, perspective, complaint, photograph, or mini-documentary via a media channel onto the Internet. As of this writing, almost 2 billion people have access to the Web's almost 300 million Web sites. Smartphone penetration is growing every day, especially across Asia, and many industry experts believe that handheld devices will someday become the dominant source of consumer news and information. News and controversy travel electronically fast. An oil spill off the coast of France can result in a speedily organized boycott of a multinational's U.S. gas stations. A front-page *New York Times* report on the working conditions in a Chinese factory can damage the reputations of Apple, Hewlett-Packard (HP), Samsung, and Microsoft. When you and I as consumers have a platform to make our feelings known, to leave positive and negative reviews about small and large businesses, and even to upload a short video of our mistreatment at a fast-food chain, secrecy becomes a relic of the past. Does this mean companies have to divulge everything? Of course not. But the era when a company could turn its back on negative publicity, or use legal threats to silence or stanch consumer or public opinion, is over. A single blogger who takes aim at corporate malfeasance can swiftly turn into a dozen bloggers, and from there, into a national movement.

Free unfettered access to public and private information is part of modern life. Information that today's employees need to manage their lives, succeed in school, or land a good job, is now readily available online any time of the day. Today's young knowledge workers expect not only to be able to voice their opinion, informed or not, on every subject but also to be informed about the activities and health of their employer and to be given the chance to provide input. What they want, ultimately, is an organization whose communication is closer to the academic model than to the Alpha business model.

If there's any company out there that's not grappling with its social media policies, I don't know about it. Should all employees be permitted to tweet? Should a single company representative be tasked with tweeting? If so, should higher-ups clear that communication first? I believe all employees have the right to communicate. Yes, there are times when businesses need to keep their private affairs close to the vest, especially where competitive advantage is concerned. But companies can no longer control or govern what their employees know. I could walk into a company tomorrow and announce a complete company reorganization, but you know what? To most employees, this news will come as no surprise. Many will have already intuited or suspected a reorg based on clues, hints, unusual behaviors, passing remarks, or even the appearance of strangers in the elevator.

I recently coached the CEO of a large company that was in the process of being sold. Though he couldn't divulge the names of his possible suitors, I urged him to meet regularly with employees, and to be as transparent as possible. Assembling his staff, the CEO told them he was in meetings with investment bankers, who were assessing the company's options. To the extent that he could share information with his employees, he promised he would. First, though, he wanted to assure everyone that the company's ability to grow, and out to scale, was at the heart of the potential sale. "Regardless of who ends up owning us," he said, "we are meeting with bankers because we are a leader in our industry, and in order to grow even more, and reach our potential, we need to bring in additional capital."

After taking questions, he set up some ground rules for employee communications. Over the next few months, employees would hear a lot of internal chatter, but the company had an official policy of never commenting publicly to the media. Until further notice, he asked employees to refrain from tweeting, and even from sharing information about the company sale with family members. In conclusion, he said, "What is relevant for you to know is how highly I value all of you—and that I am selling the company because it is best for all of us, collectively."

Again, if he had said nothing, and conducted company business behind closed doors, would his employees have known something was up? Of course. When a team of bankers shows up in an executive suite only to vanish inside a closed-door conference room, or a colleague blurts out that he caught sight of a memo featuring the names of several investment and mergers-and-acquisitions firms, it's obvious to everyone that something is taking place at the upper levels of a company.

A consumer products company once called me in to help find a successor to the sixty-two-year-old company CEO, who had announced his retirement at the end of the year. Not surprisingly, I would be auditioning for the job against a handful of corporate executive search firms. Generally speaking, in similar scenarios, search firm reps make a formal presentation, before reeling off a list of high-profile candidates they believe would be good matches for the CEO job. But when it was my turn to address the board, I flipped the paradigm around. "I'm pretty sure you have already had meetings with other firms," I began. "I'm also pretty sure that the people from those firms marched in here and said, 'Hey—I know this perfect person and that perfect person, and if you hire our search firm, we'll get a new person in place in no time at all." I paused. "No doubt you're expecting me to do the exact same thing."

Instead, I asked them to put on the brakes and think for a moment. The organization, I pointed out, was not even remotely ready to begin its search for a successor to the CEO.

Everyone on the board looked surprised. How did I know that? I had just walked in off the street. It wasn't as though I knew anyone in the organization.

In response, I told them I wanted to ask a simple question: How had the company reached a point in its evolution where there was no successor waiting in the wings who was familiar with the corporate culture? Why were there no processes in place? What made the hiring committee so positive that the organization would automatically accept and embrace an outside candidate? Of course I could give them the names of any number of possible successors from outside the firm, but was that really the issue here?

"What I *can* sell you," I said, "is not an executive search, but instead, a comprehensive *pre*-search." Along with the in-house search committee, I told the CEO that we would work together to ensure that everyone in the organization had a hand in finding and choosing an appropriate successor. New leaders were disruptive, I didn't have to remind the board. Neither was I averse to bringing in an outsider, but first the board had to do its homework and analysis. The last thing any of us wanted or needed was the corporate equivalent of an organ rejection. "Bringing in an outsider who lacks even the slightest understanding of the company or its culture," I reminded them, "will end up setting this company back a year."

They hired me, and we began a consulting relationship. I sat down with the management team, and eventually with the company's employees. The CEO was retiring, I said, and my mission was to address the staff as a group and as individuals. Together we would assess what the next generation of leadership at the company might look like, and I also made it clear that the CEO position was open to any employee willing to compete for the job.

I spent two weeks inside that company. I met with countless employees. I absorbed a lot of valuable input. Ultimately, two long-time employees, a COO and the head of sales and marketing, decided to compete for the CEO job with an outside candidate. When talking with them, I realized that neither one was the complete package. Together we not only redefined the future organizational roles these employees could take on, but we agreed to increase their compensation. I also convinced the retiring CEO to stay on at the company for another year, so he could prepare his successor for the future, which included a rumored acquisition. When the company was finally bought out, the company had a fantastic candidate at its helm who knew the company culture inside and out, and who could acclimate the new owners to the dynamics of the corporate environment. Best of all, the three candidates—two internal, and one external—felt as though they were equals, colleagues, and collaborators. Shared responsibilities, shared compensation—that's Beta.

As I mentioned earlier, companies hold tight to secrets even when they don't need to. In contrast, Beta companies generally trust that they are staffed by grown-ups. Therefore, if an issue doesn't involve a proprietary or competitive threat, why not engage your employees around the topic by allowing them to help brainstorm possible solutions? Why conceal information from the very people who will have to live with the results of that hidden information? Once employees confront a closed-door culture—literally or figuratively—it's no longer about the business; it's about the leader. (A company can barricade as many doors as it wants, as long as its culture is engaged, transparent, and communicative.)

External communication isn't much better in many Alpha organizations. There, typically the only feedback that counts is sales data and metrics. These organizations often go out of their way to evade post-transaction communications with their clients and customers. Some Alpha companies shield themselves behind hard-to-navigate phone systems or bureaucracies, to the point of actually concealing contact information on their Web sites. Reviewers and journalists are treated with suspicion. In some consumer goods companies, information about ingredients, components, and processes is kept secret from consumers, and pricing can be obscured by extra fees and hidden charges. These companies enmeshed in an Industrial Age culture seldom communicate with competitors other than via marketing challenges.

In the Information Age, this tightly controlled communication flow has to change, or organizations will be left behind. Beta companies know that communication is a resource that should be harvested constantly and used freely. They recognize that the connectivity they have with their employers, suppliers, customers, and even their competitors is a prime corporate asset. Which is why they facilitate and encourage communication.

"You can't just say you care what people think," says Gerry Lopez, the CEO and president of AMC Entertainment Holdings, Inc. "You have to mean it. Younger people today demand authenticity from their leaders. They can spot if you are a bluffer very quickly. If you offer them slick explanations and try to spin them, they'll see through it right away. The more courageous ones will call you on it. The rest will just write you off."

This may mean you have to make the same points over and over again, says Jon Miller investor and an executive visionary in the digital industry. "People won't believe you if you say something once. You have to say it a thousand times, and then follow through and actually do what you say you're going to do. It's only through this cumulative kind of effort that the message gets accepted. You have to be present in the company, both physically and as part of its electronic culture, so employees can see you understand things from their point of view, as well as your own."

And you have to do more than just say you understand and appreciate your employees. You have to show it, too. "Knowledge industry workers today, whatever their job, want to feel and be treated like principals rather than worker bees," says Jon Miller. "Materially that can mean getting stock options, but it also means they want to work hard and feel like they have a role in the decision-making and direction-setting of the company. That's far different from the way employees in a command-and-control environment felt. They were comfortable with being told what to do. In today's information technology world, in which most senior executives are far removed from the actual products, it's essential [that] those who do have direct impact on the product are able to feel that sense of ownership."

Of course, educating and informing can go too far, Fred Wilson adds. Improved communication doesn't mean that Beta leaders can or should abdicate their responsibilities. "There's a difference between informing and empowering. You can't turn a company into a democracy," Wilson says. "Some people think if they shout loud and long enough, they'll change your opinion. The rank and file should have all the information, should be encouraged to talk to their managers, and that should filter up to the CEO through the senior leadership team. But ultimately, the CEO still has to make the decision."

For the company's sake, it's also vital that people understand the responsibilities that accompany "ownership." "The quid pro quo for having 'ownership' is acting like a principal," says Jon Miller.

"Principals don't deliver problems, they solve problems. Managers, if they're going to be treated like principals, need to not just identify problems and pass them along to senior management. They need to make decisions and solve problems themselves."

Just as IT-empowered employees want to have at the very least a voice in their companies' operations, so customers want to be treated as more than just passive sources of revenue. In today's environment, customers are demanding more than just a financial relationship. Or as I like to put it, customers need to be *told,* rather than *sold.*

Since information technology provides consumers with the ability to compare prices and shop from any number of suppliers from around the globe, customers are demanding that their suppliers also provide information and advice, not just product. Companies address this in part by allowing customers the freedom to write reviews that *other* potential customers can study and review. Sometimes that's still not enough. Customers may also expect to be educated about everything from the sourcing and manufacture of products and services to their best applications and uses. Alpha companies were traditionally adept at the hard sell. Beta companies need to become expert at the soft sell: a subtle, casual, informational pitch.

A company needn't be high-tech to transform itself into a source of information for its customers. There's no better example of this kind of relationship than the Butterball Turkey Talk Line. For the past three deacades, Butterball has staffed a toll-free hotline in November and December that allows consumers to get advice on all things related to cooking a turkey-based holiday meal. It makes no difference if the person calling is preparing a Butterball turkey or some other brand. By becoming a source of expertise not just for company advice but for top-of-the-line know-how on cooking turkeys in general, Butterball has become the most recognizable name in the industry. The goodwill and positive publicity engendered by the Talk Line have more than compensated the company for the costs of providing consumer advice and guidance. Any customer who contacts the Talk Line for help feels that the successful Thanksgiving dinner she's about to prepare is a collaborative effort between her and the company. And isn't collaborative effort an essential component of Beta?

The Alpha paradigm is all about the individual. In the business world, it's the Jack Welch–style CEO standing atop the corporate pyramid. At home, it's the classic, 1950s-style dad who is king of his castle. In sports, it's the Michael Jordan–level superstar who puts the team on his back and carries it to victory, almost entirely on his shoulders. And in the arts, it's the domineering film director whose vision dictates every aspect of the creative process. We can even see the Alpha paradigm as an integral component of America's historic movements toward isolationism, exceptionalism, and libertarianism. For better or for worse, the United States has often self-identified as *the* Alpha nation. But in today's flat global economy, going it alone doesn't work.

Back in the days when human beings were hunter-gatherers who inhabited small settlements, we didn't worry about how our investments were faring, whether our daughter would get into Yale or Princeton, how the board would respond to our suggested acquisition or whether or not the car repairs would be completed by the time we got home from work. The owner of a general store in a rural setting didn't worry whether his Web presence was optimized on Google, if his China-based supplier was building safe products, if his software was providing reliable data on sales and inventory, or if his customers were spreading negative reviews on Yelp.

What makes today so different is the way information technology has radically increased the acceleration of this complexity. Moore's law says that the speed and capacity of every element of information technology grows exponentially. This remarkably accurate theory inspired author and futurist Ray Kurzweil's 2001 essay, "The Law of Accelerating Returns," in which he argued that, "We won't experience 100 years of progress in the twenty-first century—it will be more like 20,000 years of progress [at today's rate]."[2]

Technology isn't the only thing that's changing at the warp-speed of sound. Social mores are also evolving with shocking speed. Attitudes toward gender roles, race, religion, and sexual preference are shifting faster than the legal and political systems can respond. Cultural tastes are more mercurial than ever. In a YouTube era, Andy Warhol's tongue-in-cheek comment that someday everybody would be famous for fifteen minutes now seems prescient, even if by today's standards, fifteen minutes seems like an eternity.

Along with this unprecedented velocity of change, organizations have to turn their focus beyond local, regional, and national factors. The rest of the globe matters. Once upon a time, a business might have concerned itself only with the quality of the local school system, the strength of the regional infrastructure, and national tax policies. Today, it must also grapple with the overall mood of French consumers and Chinese technocrats. In an anxious, unsettled world, maintaining a global focus is essential. However deranged mutually assured destruction sounded to most of us, the Cold War's balance of power ultimately stabilized the planet. Ever since the Soviet Union dissolved, the world has fractured into chaos as countries come apart and non-state elements (terrorists, pirates, drug cartels, crime lords) rush in to fill the vacuums.

All of which makes it even more difficult, if not impossible, for a single person, or even a dedicated group, to have all the answers. With the tempo so stepped up, the risk of relying on one person, or even a small insular group, for expertise and guidance is far too great. Miss an opportunity to enter an emerging market or industry, and your company could end up in financial straits. Today, as I wrote earlier, it takes two people and any number of support systems to run a household and family—just as it takes three superstars to win an NBA championship. And it takes collaborative effort, involving input from all its constituents, for a business to succeed.

What could be more archaic and counterproductive than the Alpha business paradigm of pitting individuals, teams, and divisions against one another in internal competition? Think about it: the more that employees focus on competing against their co-workers, the less they're able to focus on competing against genuine rivals: other companies.

Whether via the creation of ad hoc teams and project-specific task forces, or the simple day-to-day encouragement of creative interaction, leaders and organizations need to maximize their intellectual resources to deal with the growing complexities of the new global economy. Bosses and employees need to work together to solve problems and accomplish shared organizational and communal goals. Not to put too fine a point on it, but they need to *collaborate*. The more collaborative opportunities a business offers its employees, the more those employees will feel a sense of ownership in the organization, resulting in vastly higher levels of productivity, efficiency, and loyalty.

One good way to ensure the development of a broad range of ideas is for senior managers to engage actively with both junior management and front-line personnel. When a company's COO or CEO takes the time to attend lower-level strategy sessions, and solicit and take note of the ideas of junior employees, it conveys the message that upper management acknowledges that the best ideas can come from the most unexpected places. In meetings, Howard Schultz, the CEO of Starbucks, is known for asking the most junior person—typically a young assistant wary about taking a seat at the conference table—what he or she thinks the best approach would be. Schultz then asks that person to explain why, giving the young assistant the same focused attention he gives to everyone else in the room. This kind of leadership gesture conveys a powerful message to every level of an organization that everyone's opinion matters.

Promoting a collaborative approach also means that Beta leaders need to approach recruiting differently. When looking for thoughtful individuals—and not just followers—it's important to look for people who are confident, willing to think outside the box, and eager to take a share in the intellectual ownership of the organization. When looking for someone who can provide ideas, not just follow orders, a person's history of creativity and innovation can be just as important as their measurable achievements. Diversity of thought will provide the spark that ignites innovation and creativity. Think about it: When everyone sees and thinks about the world the same way, just about everyone will come up with the same answers and approaches. Today, that kind of tunnel vision is a recipe for disaster.

"One of the big challenges I faced when I first took the job here," says Gerry Lopez of AMC Entertainment Holdings, Inc.,

was to diversify the talent. I don't mean racially or ethnically. I mean diversity of thought, style, approach, and background. I didn't want to have twelve direct reports, all of whom had the same background and experience. I wanted different human beings so we had some kind of balance, rather than a dozen people who all think the same. We identified some of the skill sets we needed to add, and brought brand-new people in from the outside. Now we have people who just arrived working with people who have been with the company for thirty years. I love that we now have that kind of balance."

Besides avoiding tunnel vision in their recruiting, Beta leaders also need to be wary of hiring only superstars. A Beta organization needs individuals who are willing to focus their creativity on achieving organizational, and not just individual, goals. The Beta leader is like the general manager of a sports franchise trying to assemble a winning team. Sure, it's tempting to go out and recruit an all-star for every position, and just as tempting to assume that a fieldful of superstars will translate into a victorious team. But have you ever watched an NBA All-Star team? It's a bunch of Alpha males taking impossible shots, not bothering to pass the ball to their teammates, and showing off for the crowd. Winning teams may require stars, but they also require role players. There's only one ball; and not everyone can run with it at the same time. Rather than constantly trying to upstage one another, people have to play their parts to the best of their abilities in order to win—and here I'm talking about sports *and* business.

"The loneliest feeling in the world has to be when you score a touchdown and you turn around and the other ten guys aren't rushing to celebrate with you," says Lopez. "You don't win alone. You have to make sure you recognize those who enabled it and contributed to it, because you didn't do it yourself. Find talent, give it an environment in which to flourish, and give it a chance to fail . . . at least once. The role I most enjoy playing is blocking back: giving someone junior the opportunity to become great."

The Beta collaborative model should also include customers. The potential for customers to serve as sources for instant feedback and creative input has been adopted widely across the software industry. Aside from offering avenues for communication, software providers are today actively soliciting from users suggestions for product changes and adaptations. The goal: to create a product community where communication and collaboration unite to create a product that constantly evolves to match the changing needs of its users and of the marketplace. When customers feel that they're not just being heard, but also have a genuine impact on product development and evolution, they become not just loyal buyers, but active promoters and company and brand ambassadors, too.

Consider the way Dove transformed its relationship with its global customers back in 2004. In a world where most females come nowhere close to size 2, Dove directly addressed the fantasies and realities of the beauty business. After all, many young women today know what cosmetic "airbrushing" is, and more than one celebrity and stylist has publicly admitted that the models on the covers of *Vogue* or *Harper's Bazaar* have been touched up, firmed, de-wrinkled, and smoothed of flab, cellulite, and signs of age. Dove researchers found that only 2 percent of women across the globe felt comfortable describing themselves as "beautiful." Which meant that 98 percent of women believed their appearance came up short.

Enter Dove's "Campaign for Real Beauty," which called on "real" women of all ages, shapes, and sizes to appear in the company's print and media advertising platforms. By targeting widespread, traditional, and unrealistic perceptions of beauty, and simultaneously inspiring females to take better care of their skin, Dove's Campaign for Real Beauty was a huge global success. Thanks to its slogan, "Real Women Have Curves," the company helped redefine what natural, un-airbrushed females really look like. Unusual among ad campaigns, the Real Beauty initiative inspired discussion in school classrooms, colleges, universities, and on TV. The company even launched the Dove Self-Esteem Fund, dedicated to raising awareness among young women about unrealistic cultural perceptions of female beauty. *The Today Show,* CNN, and *The Oprah Winfrey Show* were among the many media outlets that devoted segments to the "real women" who appeared on billboards and in print ads to support Dove's initiative. By listening to what female consumers had to say about their appearance, Dove collaborated with the girls and women of the world to yank back the curtain on the beauty and fashion industry, and reestablish new definitions of "beautiful."

Another company that listens to its consumers is Weight Watchers, which today operates in thirty countries. Via research and focus groups, the company figured out that overweight men generally resist joining community support networks or members meetings. Yet the company also found that far more than women, men were likely to use Weight Watchers' iPhone and Android apps. "Although we are predominantly female, we do have a decent percentage of men following the program," said Chief Marketing Officer Cheryl Callan in an interview with *Advertising Age*. Since Weight Watchers launched its men-only Web site, and hired former NBA star Charles Barkley, "We've seen a lot more male success stories come though."[3]

No company's attempt to bring consumers into its fold would be complete without mentioning Pepsi's 2010 "Pepsi Refresh" initiative. Arguably the biggest social media campaign ever created by a major corporation, Pepsi Refresh leveraged contemporary thinking—and contemporary tools—to unleash community action. The rules were very simple: consumers could apply for grants ranging from $5,000 to $250,000 in any one of a half-dozen categories: health, arts and culture, the planet, food and shelter, and neighborhoods and education. Pepsi engaged consumers via a large online distribution system, including Facebook, Twitter, YouTube, and the company's own Web site. Roughly one thousand applications flooded Pepsi's offices monthly, and consumers voted on the ones they deemed most worthwhile. Among the grant winners were a group who provided care packages for overseas U.S. troops, an initiative focused on improving literacy in local Atlanta high schools, even a fourteen-year-old boy whose goal was to make school buses more energy-efficient. In one year, Pepsi gave away roughly $20 million.

It's worth repeating: In an era of conversational media, consumer and employees alike want to be *told,* not *sold.* They want to be educated, to engage in genuine conversations. Recently, I've been helping a number of companies create customer advisory boards made up of actual consumers who have "liked" a company or its products and services on Facebook. My goal in creating these boards is to bring in real-life people to discuss an organization from a consumer perspective, and determine what the company, product or service could do better. I've also been working in tandem with a business that sells point-of-sale software. Thus, if you are in the habit of ordering a Starbucks mocha latte at 5:00 P.M. every afternoon, you could text your nearest Starbucks to remind them to have your latte waiting for you when you show up. In turn, the store might text you back, "There's a longer line than we expected today, which means we'll have your latte ready for you at 5:15." If that doesn't sound like a conversation between a company and a consumer, well, I don't know what does.

Today, Beta business leaders are even pursuing collaborative efforts with potential competitors in order to leverage their capabilities and decrease their risks. Consider how Hulu, the ad-supported streaming video Web site, got its start. A handful of television studios and networks realized that the future of their businesses included downloadable and streaming content. Individually, no one in this group had the internal expertise or market share to dominate this emerging business. Yet none of them could afford to ignore what was likely to become a significant future distribution channel.

So NBC Universal (General Electric/Vivendi), Fox Entertainment Group (News Corp.), and ABC, Inc. (The Walt Disney Company) took the unprecedented step of collaborating. Thanks to funding from Providence Equity Partners, the companies launched Hulu. Regardless of the long-term financial success of the venture, Hulu has enabled three rival businesses to become players in a crucial market that none was equipped to navigate alone. What's more, competitor/partner relationships are becoming more common. Just look at the shifting collaborations and alliances between firms like Apple, Google, Amazon, and Microsoft, who have sometimes joined forces and other times fought fiercely, only to begin the process all over again.

Collaborations between competitors, or between companies and users, are nothing for either progressives or conservatives to fear. They're neither precursors to socialism nor impending cartels. Nor are they attempts to score free labor. Collaborations reflect nothing more than the complexity of today's business world. They are simply intelligent alliances aimed at building a community to help solve mutual problems and achieve shared goals.

Alpha leaders are commanders; they issue orders to their subordinates. In an Alpha organization, strategizing, planning, and decision-making are centralized, often in the guise of a single executive, whether he goes by the name of CEO, owner, director, or chairman. There may be a small elite group that is theoretically empowered to advise and consult with the boss, but whether it's the board of directors, a management committee, a kitchen cabinet, or a privy council, few constituents can truly influence an Alpha leader. In extreme cases, these groups serve as little more than rubber stamps for the Alpha, their indirect mission being to make an autocracy come across as an oligarchy.

The CEO job is an isolated and increasingly short-lived position. In a 2012 study of the world's 2,500 largest public companies, consultants Booz & Company found that the average job tenure for a CEO is 6.6 years. By way of illustrating how cut off most CEOs are, I'll tell you a story. In my office, over my desk, I keep a beautiful painting that shows a wintry, tundralike landscape. Snow is everywhere, covering a pair of mountain peaks and a fallen tree. In the foreground is a solitary male figure (he looks a little like the actor Gregory Peck) carrying two suitcases. Whenever I counsel CEOs or leaders in my office, at some point I always say, "What you're describing reminds me of that picture on my wall." My visitors glance over my shoulder. "What do you see in that picture, anyway?" I ask.

What these high-powered leaders confess in the next five minutes tells me more about them, and what's *really* happening in their work lives, than I could uncover in ten hours of conversation. One CEO told me that the man in the picture was running for his life. Another CEO told me the man was slowly making his way toward future opportunities. Others have told me that the man is alone on a limb, that he's lost his way, and that the bridge behind him has washed out, obliging him to hike through the woods with no trail ahead. Some perceive the landscape positively—*he's going skiing!*—while others see only aggravation and misfortune. As I look back on all these various narratives and scenarios, I'm always struck by how often the words *lonely* and *alone* come up. It's as if they are all saying, in various ways, *The man in the picture knows where he is going. But ultimately he is alone. He can ask others to follow or accompany him, but at the end of the day, he is still by himself.*

"So *why* is the man out there all alone?" I reply. "Why doesn't he have people with him? What if he had a team behind him? Would it be any harder for him? Would it be any easier?"

By now it's obvious that the landscape over my desk is a mini-Rorschach test that provokes and stimulates conversation in ways normal conversation wouldn't. Without making my point overtly, the leaders I counsel and I can agree: The CEO's journey is a solitary one. Most leaders lack all perspective. They trust practically no one in the organization. Yet at the same time, there are no leaders without followers—which is why collaborating with and inspiring others to accompany leaders on their journey is the only way to go. Otherwise, leaders run the risk of losing sight of their true north or, worse, getting their heads chopped off.

But considering that many autocratic CEOs manage by fear and fiat, this can be a difficult transition for an Alpha leader to make. I once worked for a CEO who, convinced that keeping employees off balance brought out the best in them, enjoyed pitting his top players against each other. The CEO then sat back, watched the battle unfold, and waited to see who came out the victor. (Think *Hunger Games,* corporate division.) I know this for a fact because at the time, I was one of those two top players. The other was a man we'll call "Stewart." One day, during my first few months in the company, there was an all-morning think tank, followed by a lunch meeting. Before going into the meeting, I freshened up, washed my hands and face, and applied some new lipstick. As I was leaving the restroom, I ran into Stewart. "Wow," he said, sounding both amused and derisive. "You've prettied yourself up for the meeting."

I pulled him aside. "Don't you ever talk to me like that," I said. "If you want to start calling out the differences between us, it would be the easiest thing in the world for me to do. But what you just said was completely unnecessary. It has nothing to do with competence. And if you want to compete on competence, I would be more than glad to do so."

Okay, I admit, at the time I was a little defensive. But it just goes to show you the level of tension and arch-competition between the two of us that the CEO had fostered.

Several weeks later, Stewart and I found ourselves sitting near each other during a long train trip to Washington. He and I started talking. In the course of our conversation, he mentioned he had two daughters, and I remember telling him, "One of the reasons I work as hard as I do, and try to set such an example to other working women, is that I want your daughters to have an easier time of it when they come into the workforce." Women in the workplace were a reality for our generation, I added, just as they would continue to be a reality in the future.

He had never thought about it that way, he told me, or for that matter how difficult it was for me to be among the first generation of women who aspired to professional success. We talked for a long time. About family. About business. It turned out we had a lot in common. As we dug deeper, both of us realized that the other was privy to precisely one-half of the overall information necessary to make our jobs, and our division, work at an optimal level. By the end of the trip, I finally came out with it: Did Stewart ever feel that he and I were competing against each other—and that that was the wrong game for the two of us to play? Did he ever feel that our mutual boss was raising our anxiety to such an extent that it was impeding the free flow of ideas, and keeping us from doing our best and what was best for the company?

I proposed a cease-fire, and a pact: What if from that point on, Stewart and I collaborated to show our boss the power of collaboration? What if no matter how things played out, we agreed to take joint credit and share all our responsibilities and obligations? "Would you buy into that?" I asked. He would. And from that day on, he and I were the company's go-to team. Observing close-up what the yin-yang of a male-female team could accomplish, the CEO proceeded to give us even choicer assignments. Sure, now and again, Stewart would slip into lone wolf mode, and I had to say, "Uh-oh, are we competing against each other again?" But I'm happy to say we both had a sense of humor about it.

As I wrote earlier, many in today's workforce came of age in untraditional families. They were the children of divorce; or they were raised by blended families; or they had two mothers, or two fathers. A few decades ago, an autocratic boss could easily manage younger workers who came from conventional family backgrounds, but as we evolve into the twenty-first century, that paradigm, and that generation of workers, no longer exists.

Careers in Alpha organizations are regimented; they follow predetermined patterns. That's because there's a clearly delineated route to the top, and everyone is told they have to strive to summit or else they're a failure. Imagine that over the course of its history, a large Alpha corporation has placed a priority on marketing. It has traditionally promoted men and women from that branch to the corner office. Therefore, the most expeditious career plan would be to get aboard the marketing track, right? If this were the case, department heads within the organization would prioritize their marketing efforts, hoping to translate their initiatives into a promotion to a job as a divisional or regional marketer. From there, they could ascend the division's marketing track and, ultimately, assume a position in the corporate-wide or national marketing arm. Once they became a member of the national team, they would play politics to the best of their ability to climb further up the ladder in order to position themselves for promotion to the upper levels of management. Which is a long way of saying that, in my experience, individuals in Alpha organizations frequently concentrate on developing the skills and achievements necessary to climb the rungs on a professional ladder favored by the existing leadership.

There's only one problem, and it's a big one. This predestined Alpha path often leads to frustration and unhappiness, and the reasons why are clear: No one has ever bothered to figure out where a person's skill set lies. As the Peter Principle famously points out, "In a hierarchy, every employee tends to rise to his level of incompetence." I once coached the president of a mid- to large-size company, a man whose career was so time-consuming, it destroyed his first marriage. Yet he was still hungry for status and position: he wanted, he said, to be named CEO of a huge global brand. Now, this man's company was large, but it had very little international reach.

"So how do I get to where I want to go, Dr. D?" he asked.

For the next several hours, we inventoried his skills, and discussed what he could do to enhance his profile. Together we mapped out an incremental five-year plan. He needed to travel, network intensively, and if possible, cajole an invitation to the World Economic Forum's yearly meeting in Davos, Switzerland. On the home front, he needed to set up international distribution inside his own company to showcase his management skills. Which he did. Over the next three years, he evolved his company into a highly influential global presence. Then one day my cell phone rang, and it was him, inviting me out to dinner.

"Okay," I said when we took a seat in the restaurant. "I can't stand the suspense anymore. What are you doing, and where are you going?"

Turns out he wasn't going anywhere.

He owed me a debt of gratitude, he said. The thing is, he thought he had to leave where he was to get what he wanted; but when he reflected back on our coaching session, he realized he could get exactly what he wanted, and more, by staying where he was. Managing a bigger company, he'd come to realize, wasn't the same as managing a *better* company. Strengthening and deepening his relationship with his employees could only make him a happier, more productive person. He and his second wife were also the new parents of twins. "I want to be present for my kids," he said, adding, "I *know* I'm good at my job. I'm making a lot of money, but right now my ego is invested in making my marriage and my family a success." Happiness, he now knew, wasn't about taking on a new high-profile position that was bigger for the sake of being bigger. He was not saying he would remain with the company forever. But right now he was where he needed to be.

The increased communication and collaboration required of Beta organizations demand a new style of leadership and career planning.

Beta leaders need to be curators, not commanders. Rather than striving to be content experts on every aspect of their operation, they need to be able to collect, sort, analyze data, and edit all communication and collaborative streams of information that could potentially influence their business. Organizations need to have dozens, maybe hundreds, of individual experts, fully capable of idea generation and innovative thought. In turn, these experts must be encouraged to drill down deep in their own specializations, develop plans and strategies, and share them with the rest of the organization. Beta leaders then need to sort through the ideas, figure out how they fit together, and then recombine them so the whole is greater than the sum of its parts.

As curators, Beta leaders are skilled at assembling employees, encouraging them to think new thoughts in different ways, and challenging them to do new things. Example: The senior executive at a major cosmetics company reinvigorated the notion of an "idea box" for her employees by placing a Hermès purse in a central location. Now, the idea box is a retro notion that few of us would ever associate with an upscale modern cosmetics company. But the Hermès purse? That was borderline-genius. (As a woman, the executive knew very well that the stuff inside a woman's handbag *matters*—that using it signaled to her staff that their feedback was not only welcome but essential.) The Idea Box turned out to be a big success, both for engaging employee buy-in, and introducing new and invigorating concepts and initiatives to the company.

Another CEO I counsel keeps a notebook on his desk with the heading WHAT MAKES YOU HAPPY? Whenever he hires new employees, he makes it a point to find out about their interests and passions, which he then documents in his notebook. Whenever employees do something the CEO wants to recognize publicly, he awards them something that dovetails with their interests and passions. Is the employee a theater nut? He'll give her two tickets to a new, sold-out Broadway show. Is the employee a basketball fan? He'll hand him a pair of third-row tickets for a New York Knicks game the following week. Is the employee a doting but frayed new parent? He'll give her a night out on the town with her husband or partner, plus babysitter money. It's a fantastic way not just to make his employees feel seen, heard, and rewarded, but to inject a little fun into the culture as well.

Again, *curating* means knowing which people to put together. It means knowing how to mix and match. It means knowing when things, or people, or teams, are getting tired, and sometimes even bringing in an outsider to shake things up.

The curatorial Beta leader gives context to the varied concepts of others, and then designs a narrative from the creativity of all the organization's thought leaders. The Beta leader next communicates the whole story to everyone who has shared in its creation. By doing so, the leader becomes the keeper of the entire organization's cultural heritage. Consider how a museum curator carefully selects individual works of art from a museum's permanent collection and borrows others from private collectors, with an overall theme in mind. She then arranges the artworks in a way that tells a story to everyone who visits the galleries. Again, it's worth thinking of the curatorial leader as akin to a symphony conductor. The conductor doesn't write the music or play an instrument, but through his direction he brings together the individual creative efforts of a hundred musicians into a thematically unified performance. By contrast, the Alpha leader, or creator, is a one-man band.

"There's definitely a generational and cultural shift taking place," says Jon Miller. "I don't feel like I need to be the general leading a command-and-control organization. I think of myself in my role of leader as the person who's throwing the party and making sure the party keeps going and stays in bounds. That doesn't mean I need to be the life of the party or the focus of the celebration," he goes on. "I don't mind others being celebrated. It's my job to move the company in a particular direction, and to convey to others that they can be the life of the party sometimes as long as they stay within the bounds I've set."

Beta Boards of Directors need to adapt a more curatorial approach as well. Today, innovation is one degree of separation from the product level. Consequently, it's difficult for board members and other high-level executives to develop sufficiently nuanced instincts to provide guidance on product decisions. Instead of trying to educate board members on the minutiae, executives need to figure out what the board needs to know to help them become more effective advisors. As Jon Miller puts it, "The old style of working with the Board was to go to them and say, 'This is what I want to do, and if you don't agree, you have to fire me because it's clear we're not in alignment.' Today, because board members can't be as immersed in the business as senior management, executives need to create context for them so they provide valuable insights and guidance." In short, you need board members who are educable rather than expert, who are inquisitive and supportive, who reach down deep into the organization and bring their knowledge networks to add value to the company.

The Sarbanes–Oxley Act—otherwise known as SOX, or Sarbox—became law in 2002, in response to a series of accounting and corporate scandals at Enron, Tyco, Adelphia, and elsewhere. When then-president Bush signed the new legislation, he announced that no American boardroom was above or below the law. At the time, the boards of *many* companies—not just Enron and Tyco—were paying inadequate attention to compliance. Many were self-regulating. They operated on the presumption that, well, their people would do the right thing. In the wake of SOX, almost overnight many boards became full-fledged all-star teams, composed of marquee names hand-chosen from government and business. Few companies considered filling their boards with people who would challenge their businesses, import new perspectives or ways of thinking, or help enhance the CEO's skills. Instead, boards brought in people whose names, experiences, and reputations proved to shareholders that the board was upholding its fiduciary responsibility to the company.

The problem is that boards, at least across the United States, tend to be populated entirely by professional managers, past or present—or to put it another way, by Alphas. Many board members share identical skill sets with the CEO in charge of the company—in fact, many *are* past or present company leaders, who are acquainted only with the CEO, and perhaps with the CFO. It's no surprise that by their very nature, boards turn into elitist bubbles, VIP clubs that seldom consider letting in equally wise, experienced individuals who could contribute a broader variety of expertise.

Where is the diversity, the deep departmental know-how, the sense of collaboration? Instead of handpicking corporate chieftains with white-shoe credentials, why not, say, appoint a former marketing executive who could help shepherd the company toward expanding its social media initiatives, or creating an affinity program to buttress new marketing initiatives? How about a human resources expert, who could contribute her long-standing expertise in employee compensation and rewards?

While we're on the subject, where *are* all the women anyway?

According to *Forbes* magazine, GMI Ratings' Women on Boards survey revealed that as of 2012, the number of females on corporate boards stood at 12.6 percent, thereby exceeding 10 percent for the very first time in history. This sounds better than it is, especially when you compare it to the 40 percent male–female corporate board quota established by the European Union (which, admittedly, will take a decade or more to accomplish).[4] *Forbes* notes that "Over three-fifths of companies have at least one female director, but this is countered by the fact that less than a tenth of companies have three or more female directors."[5] More to the point, *Forbes* notes that countless academic studies show conclusively that diverse boards lead to a higher quality of board dialogue, decision-making and "organizational and financial performance."[6] In constast to Norway, which requires 40 percent of its board members to be women, the United States is doing poorly, though not so badly as Italy and Japan. Interestingly, the percentage of female directors at South African companies is 17.4 percent, a higher ratio than in many industrialized countries, including Australia and France. Moreover, 37 percent of all South African companies have at least three women on their boards.

Yet adding women to boards in order to achieve gender parity would make no sense if history didn't show us what females bring to the table. In a follow-up article in *Forbes* magazine, Bob Deutsch notes, "When men and women work together, their different cognitive temperaments—in alchemy and in mutual oversight—can create visions and solutions that have a better 'fit' to the current environment of complexity."[7] A business consultant and cognitive anthropologist, Deutsch has spent years exploring how people make decisions. Among his conclusions? "Women cycle, and men consummate." In general, Deutsch says, men orient themselves to practical and pragmatic solutions. Their focus is on winning. In contrast, women are "oriented to the conceptual, to underlying dynamics, to the relationship between things, and to stability over the long-term."[8] Women grasp patterns, movements, and mutations more easily than men. If male leaders veer toward achievement-oriented, command-and-control philosophies, women emphasize evolvement, experience, and strong relationships. Says Deutsch, "Mixed male and female groups who combine the different gender-based ways of perceiving causality, time and power, tend to compose better problem-structuring and problem-solving entities compared with same-sex groups. . . . Together males and females are better than each separately. They could help each other bring out the best in the boardroom."[9]

It's time for the pendulum to swing in the other direction. Boards were originally created to sit at a CEO's knees—not to sit in counsel of the shareholders. (Of course, if the board carries them out properly, these two missions are one and the same.) If a board focuses exclusively on the CEO, it risks overlooking everyone else in the company. It dodges its responsibility of helping steer the ship and set future policy. Rather than addressing the usual questions, such as for example, *What does the CEO need? How can we enhance everyone in the company?* Boards should instead confront questions like, *What is this board for in the first place? What does the community need from this board? Is there anyone here from human resources who could serve as an advocate for the employees?*

Instead of acting like a police force, boards need to recapture the advisory role they had before the Sarbanes–Oxley bill became law. With its cumulative experience, a board could coalesce theories, advice, ideas, and guidance, and serve as an unofficial think tank for the CEO. Union Square Ventures' Fred Wilson encourages CEOs to surround themselves with supportive board members. "A lot of CEOs are criticized for stacking their boards, getting people who will just serve as rubber stamps. But it's important for management to have a board that's in sync with its management style

and vision. Nothing drives a CEO crazier than having an unsup-
portive board. Mismatched CEO and boards are like bad
marriages."

Beta companies should focus on recruiting board members who
offer more than just technical wisdom. There should be board members who can provide input on strategy and corporate culture, not
just on financial issues. As an interim step to shifting board membership, some Beta CEOs are hiring consultants to serve in a consigliere role.

Beta careers need to be curated, too. Rather than narrowly
concentrating professional development inside an organization based
on the skills and experiences that fit a prescribed pattern, individuals need to develop patterns that match their needs and wants. In
Beta organizations, employees can pursue their own path by looking at what they love, what they do well, and what excites them.
Does what you love most fit the traditional model? No? The good
news is, it doesn't matter. In Beta organizations, there *are* no traditional models. There is no one path to the top. There is no single,
formalized definition of success. Instead, multiple paths lead to
multiple variations of success. In Beta organizations, careers are no
longer one-size-fits-all any more than corporate solutions can answer forty different organizational questions.

I recently sat down an advertising executive who is following
what I consider a Beta career path—meaning she has not bought
into the idea that changing jobs means she is making professional
progress. She knows she's building up a strong body of work and
reputation in her current job. Why move on, she said to me, when
everything I love and that motivates me is right in front of me?
Why leave a place where my colleagues and I value one another, and
where I am already getting a big slice of the pie? Let's be clear: she
wasn't saying *all* employees are better off "accepting their lot in
life." But she knew "bigger" was not necessarily "better," and that

ascending for ascension's sake, or in order to earn a few dollars more in salary, wouldn't make her any happier than she already was. There was, she told me, a lot to be said for enjoying the community around her, broadening her expertise in her current job, and a few years from now, retiring from a single institution.

Today's knowledge workers are seeking much more than material compensation. They're looking for organizations whose environments are both professionally supportive and physically comfortable. This is one reason why so many top knowledge industry companies are famous for the amenities available at their *campuses*. Incidentally, the widespread use of that word deliberately connotes the informal, iconoclastic, collaborative (and intense) environment of higher education. Make no mistake, though: incredible cafeterias, day cares, gymnasiums, and bicycles for every employee are fantastic, but they're not enough. Today's employees need and increasingly demand the opportunity to tailor their own professional development. In short, they're looking for companies that curate, rather than proscribe a one-size-fits-all path of professional development.

Example: An employee finds she's highly skilled at managing reorganizations, or departmental restructurings. The Beta approach would be for this employee to market herself as a reorganization specialist and curate a course of professional development that could lead her to any number of different organizations. She could absorb the very best information on strategies and tactics for reorganization. She could uncover the best advice on seeking out and landing such assignments. For her, the ultimate mission comes down to creating a course of professional development that matches what she wants and needs. For the organization, it comes down to providing her with whatever resources she needs in order to succeed in her chosen course.

This personalized approach to employee development not only

develops more effective Beta managers and leaders for the future, but it also strengthens the bonds between individuals and the company—an especially welcome side effect in an era when numerous employees feel alienated from their employers. There are few better ways to inspire loyalty in your people than by treating and valuing them as the individuals they are.

This is one reason why the software company Intuit is a perennial nominee for "most admired company" and "best place to work" by *Fortune* magazine. The firm's social activism—it gives employees paid time off to volunteer; matches employee charitable donations; and donates money, products, and services to nonprofits—has certainly enhanced its reputation as an exemplary workplace. But it's the company's belief that individual employees are the reason for its success that makes Intuit so popular among its people. There's no better evidence of the loyalty engendered by this approach than the fact that many employees include the company mantra "It's the People," in their personal e-mail signatures.

Shoemaker Timberland is another company that employees love to love. It might very well have to do with the emphasis that CEO Jeffrey Swartz puts on good citizenship inside and outside the company. Employees receive up to forty hours of paid leave every year to pursue volunteer projects, many of which are organized under an initiative dubbed "Serve-a-palooza," which has tackled everything from cleaning and restoring public spaces in a down-and-out New England town to enhancing a program for handicapped children in Vietnam to helping expand the reach of rural medicine in the Dominican Republic. Timberland also offers its roughly 6,000 workers a check for $3,000 toward the purchase of a hybrid automobile. Says Helen Whinfrey, Timberland's senior manager for European Human Resources, "We have a philosophy about our employees doing well and doing good. People perform better in their job if they have a connection with their work that isn't just about pay. It also means the local community knows who we are—we don't want to be a faceless business with no connection to where we work and trade. Of course we're a commercial enterprise, but we believe the way we generate profit, treat our people and work with the local community puts that profit in a different light."[10]

As a *Fast Company* article notes about Timberland and its CEO, "What Swartz is really trying to do is to use the resources, energy, and profits of a publicly traded footwear-and-apparel company to combat social ills, help the environment, and improve conditions for laborers around the globe. And rather than using his company as a charity, he's using the hard financial metrics of profit, return on investment, and shareholder return, to try to prove that doing good and doing well are actually self-reinforcing notions. The idea of helping others, Swartz believes, is a vision around which he is creating a more productive, efficient, loyal, and committed employee base, which in turn helps produce real results."[11] The good news? It's working, too.

The communicative, collaborative, and curatorial approach of Beta organizations is an ideal fit for the Information Age and today's generation of knowledge workers. In short, in today's environment, Beta offers the best opportunity for organizational success. But that isn't all that it offers. The Beta paradigm also provides individuals with a chance to achieve the emotional and psychological satisfaction that was so often lacking inside Alpha organizations.

SIX

THE TOP OF A DIFFERENT PYRAMID

Alpha children wear grey. They work much harder than
we do, because they're so frightfully clever. I'm really awfully glad
I'm a Beta, because I don't work so hard.

—ALDOUS HUXLEY, *Brave New World*

The Beta paradigm represents a modern alternative to the traditional, Industrial Age, pyramid-based hierarchy. But Beta can also symbolize ultimate fulfillment of a different, and more essential, pyramid: Maslow's hierarchy of needs.

We expend a lot of human energy on the petty matters and affairs that clog up our daily schedules. Despite these various demands—from ensuring sales quotas are met to getting the kids to school on time—from a psychological perspective an individual's greatest mission in life is to achieve what's called self-actualization. For most of us, the ultimate personal goal, the primary aim, is to uncover our full potential as human beings: to be the most fully ourselves that we can possibly be.

Self-actualization is a term familiar to everyone who took Psychology 101 in college, or who has ever had to sit through a routine marketing presentation on consumer motivation. "Self-actualization," and "What a man can be, he must be," are in fact two of the phrases coined by psychologist Abraham Maslow in the mid 1940s, that he later expanded on in his influential 1954 book, *Motivation and Personality*. Instead of studying the mentally ill or the neurotic, Maslow studied high achievers with an eye toward developing more aspirational, success-oriented ideas. What he came up with certainly provided *him* with success.

Maslow drew a now-famous pyramid graph that he dubbed the Hierarchy of Needs. At the base of the pyramid he placed what he labeled as the most fundamental of human needs. The pyramid climbed and narrowed through five levels of needs from the most elemental to the most transcendent.

In order, from the bottom up:

- First are physiological needs for air, water, food, clothing, shelter, and sex, which make up the foundation.
- The next step consists of safety needs: personal and financial security, and the health of oneself and one's loved ones.
- Third are the needs for love and belonging, which Maslow identified as being focused on relationships, either with family and friends, or with peers, coworkers, and teammates.
- Then comes esteem: the need to respect oneself, and to be respected by others.
- Finally, at the top of the pyramid, is the need for self-actualization, or as Maslow says elsewhere in his book, "A musician must make music, an artist must paint, a poet must write, if he is to be ultimately at peace with himself. What a man can be, he must be. He must be true to his own nature. This need we may call self-actualization."[1]

Maslow's theory was that individuals need to have their most basic, or "deficiency," needs met before they can focus on higher-level, or "being," needs. Those individuals positioned to achieve their highest-level needs Maslow saw as meta-motivated. While most psychological analyses of Maslow have studied his hierarchy as it applies to our personal lives, it's just as relevant to our work lives.

In the workplace, physiological needs are addressed by the physical quality of the place of business. At a core level, people need a workspace that provides them not only with shelter from the elements, but also adequate space and light and a comfortable temperature in which to work. They need functioning bathroom facilities and potable drinking water.

Safety needs in the workplace consist of more than just freedom from potential physical danger. These might also include a sense of job security, protection from unfair treatment by superiors, protections against harassment, and the safety net provided by benefits like medical, dental, life, and disability insurance.

Belonging in the workplace means feeling part of a connected group of colleagues, or a formal or informal team.

How does esteem translate to the workplace? Through the respect employees receive from employees, peers, and employers, as well as the self-respect we receive from our own competence, skill set, and productivity.

Finally, self-actualization in the workplace comes down to knowing that a company, supervisor, and position allow us to take advantage of our fullest potential, by letting us do what we enjoy, are good at, and find emotionally and psychologically fulfilling.

When it comes to meeting deficiency needs, there's little practical difference between Alpha and Beta organizations. No matter how autocratic a CEO may be, his company wouldn't be around for very long if he didn't provide an environment in which his employees were physically able to do their work. Similarly, no matter how collaborative a CEO is, she won't be able to help her employees feel satisfied on the job if their incomes are at risk or if they're forced to give up insurance protection. (While the nature of a Beta organization promotes a company-wide sense of belonging and shared purpose, there's another, more perverse sense of community that often develops among the downtrodden in any organization. Like soldiers sharing danger in a foxhole, underappreciated, put-upon employees can develop a sense of community via shared unhappiness.)

For individuals who are, in Maslow's words, meta-motivated, that is, who seek to satisfy their needs for esteem and fulfillment, the differences between working at an Alpha or Beta organization are significant. The foundations of Beta—communication, collaboration, and curation—provide the highest possible chances for employees to achieve workplace self-actualization.

An organization that encourages open communication, and whose leadership reaches out to all its constituents, demonstrates that it values every employee and every role. An organization that actively promotes collaboration shows that it respects the intelligence, ideas, and opinions of everyone. An organization that curates, rather than dictates, professional development reconfirms that it sees everyone as an individual. Employees are far more likely to have their esteem needs met in a company that actively demonstrates its respect for all by being inclusive and embracing the importance of every single employee's role and contribution. And a company that supports the notion of individuals maximizing their own singular talents, and that respects and rewards those talents, gives employees the opportunity to be everything they can be . . . and more.

Southwest Airlines founder Herb Kelleher has often spoken about Southwest's corporate culture as the glue, or connective tissue, that upholds the airline's beliefs, communication patterns, and reward structures. Kelleher must be doing something right, as Southwest has been profitable every year since he founded it in 1971. Southwest's organizational culture is predicated on three overarching themes—love, fun, and efficiency—and when the airline was at its pinnacle in the early 1980s, Kelleher not only knew the names of most of his employees, he insisted they call him "Herb" or "Herbie."

The company's Dallas headquarters are strikingly different from most corporate offices. Instead of generic corporate art, the lobby spills over with photographs of Southwest employees and news clippings about their accomplishments. The company actively encourages its employees to innovate. (Instead of a Human Resources Department, Southwest has its own proprietary People and Leadership Development Department.) The airline has long believed that if a company treats its people with respect, and gives them the space, incentive, and inspiration to do their jobs, it can create a team of brand enthusiasts and ambassadors.

Ultimately, Southwest's competitive advantage lies in its employees, who have been instrumental in creating Southwest's famously joyful, occasionally batty customer service department. As we saw earlier with JetBlue, if great customer service means that the pilot and copilot have to load bags on the tarmac to ensure Southwest's turnaround record of fifteen minutes (the industry standard is thirty-five minutes), then that's the way it goes. Southwest's all-for-one, one-for-all spirit engenders consumer trust while buttressing both employee motivation and interpersonal connectivity.

Zappos, the online shoe retailer, isn't really about sneakers, or loafers, or boat shoes, or hiking boots. At core it's about creating and sustaining an open, transparent, collaborative environment. Recognizing that a culture built around employees and their attainment of happiness can't help but trickle down to how employees interact with online consumers, CEO Tony Hsieh has made it his company's mission to focus on superlative customer service.

A candidate applying for a job at Zappos passes through two sets of interviews—the first introductory interview is followed by a second, more rigorous interview by the HR department. The big question: Will this candidate fit easily in the Zappos culture? All new hires, including Web site designers and accountants, then pass through a four-week training program that includes two weeks answering phones at a Zappos call center. As the training program winds up, Zappos famously offers all new employees two thousand dollars to quit on the spot. As CEO Hsieh sees it, the people who take the money probably wouldn't have made great Zappos employees, anyway. (The company estimates that less than 1 percent of all candidates end up accepting the cash.)

In most companies, a clear-cut chain of command dictates who can talk to whom. But at Zappos, every employee is freely encouraged to talk to everyone else. Then there are the company's ten Core Values, spelled out on the company Web site. They urge all Zappos employees to "Embrace and Drive Change," "Create Fun and a Little Weirdness," "Be Adventurous, Creative, and Open-Minded," "Pursue Growth and Learning," "Build a Positive Team and Family Spirit," "Be Passionate and Determined," and not least, "Be Humble." The upshot is that every Zappos employee—who is also given unrestricted access to social media to post about his or her experiences working there—turns into a passionate brand advocate.

Zappos has also assembled a "culture book" for all new hires detailing the experience of working there. All employee participations are accepted and compiled, and aside from obvious typos, the company doesn't censor any criticisms. The book exposes new hires to both the good and the bad of Zappos culture. "For Zappos, it was a risk worth taking," Tony Hsieh writes in his book, *Delivering Happiness*. "If the company was truly going to stand behind its culture and core values, there couldn't be a better way to see if Zappos was doing it right . . . [and] what began as an off-the-cuff idea five years ago has now become something bigger. It started as a medium where employees could freely express themselves, and a way everyone could get a pulse of where the company's culture and core values stood. Over time, we asked vendors, partners, and customers to contribute their perspective, too. Today, it's become a book of reference for anyone remotely interested in Zappos, be it as a job applicant, a small business owner, or a future entrepreneur. Above all, because the company believes culture is an essential part of its business, it has become the brand book."[2]

Zappos also publishes a monthly employee newsletter. Titled *Ask Anything,* the newsletter is just that. Every month, the company assembles the questions and answers, and e-mails them to everyone in the company. A representative sample of some of the questions that have been asked: *"Who is on the Zappos.com board of directors?" "Where do you see us in 3 years? How big, how many, and where?"* and *"How many people at Zappos.com have the same birthday and anniversary date? Any one day more than others?"*[3]

Zappos isn't merely one of the most innovative start-ups of the past decade. CEO Hsieh is also a longtime student of what makes employees, and a company, "happy."[4] To this end, he has created a loose, free-wheeling environment where managers are urged to put their feet up and shoot the breeze with the employees they manage. Several years ago, Hsieh also set up an in-house two-hundred-hour curriculum, which among other things, requires employees to read nine separate business books, and take classes in public oratory and financial planning.

3M is another company that encourages its employees to carve out time daily to pursue off-beat activities and initiatives. Like Pixar and Google, the company has even instituted a "15 percent rule," meaning that company researchers are required to spend that percentage of every day exploring new ideas, inventions, and initiatives and sharing them with their colleagues. 3M dubs this rule "Bootlegging Hour."

Another way to engage your customers is by linking your

culture to a larger cause. Founded in 1981 with just a single Vermont coffee shop, the environmentally and socially conscious Green Mountain Coffee (GMC) has created a contagious environment of openness and respect, as well as a uniform belief in sustainability so widespread that Green Mountain Coffee truck drivers turn off their engines to conserve gas every time they make a delivery. Needless to say, the culture is flat, with in-house environmental and social initiatives typically originating from the bottom up. Like all Beta companies, the culture places a premium on employee passion, believing that passions carried out passionately tend to generate great ideas *and* great business results. With its six-hundred-person workforce, jobs are divvied up into half a dozen functions: sales and marketing; operations; human resources; finance; information systems; and social responsibility. No matter what level employees are at, Green Mountain acknowledges and respects their input. Collaboration and communication are paramount, and employees are asked regularly to weigh in on the decision data that shows up on GMC's computer terminals. When the company has to make an especially important decision, Green Mountain creates what it calls a "constellation" of input, gathering ideas and opinions from all employee levels.

Inspired by its own mission statement, which aspires to give consumers the "ultimate coffee experience" while transforming how the rest of the world perceives business, every year Green Mountain flies its employees to Central America to meet company suppliers, the actual growers and workers and communities that create and supply its product. If it's a career in a socially and environmentally conscious Beta organization that you are after, Green Mountain clearly has its employees' backs.

For all its longevity and financial effectiveness over the centuries, the Alpha paradigm has generally failed to provide psychological satisfaction, much less self-actualization, to a vast majority of employees.

In fact, Alpha actually *decreases* most employees' self-esteem. All you have to do is take a look at the numbers.

For every successful Alpha, there are hundreds, and even thousands, of Betas. And if winning, or succeeding, is measured by reaching the top slot, then everyone who fails to win the ultimate prize is seen as second-best, second-rate, a runner-up, an also-ran. Charles Barkley had a Hall of Fame NBA career, but since he never won a national championship, from an Alpha perspective his legacy is severely tainted. A novelist may have written countless works of lasting value, but if she didn't make the *New York Times* bestseller list, from an Alpha perspective she is a failure. A climber may have made it to base of the Hillary Step on Mount Everest, but if he failed to summit, then from an Alpha perspective he didn't go home a winner. The Alpha paradigm has led many executives who never reached the corner office, and managers who never became top-rank executives, and front-line workers who never became managers, to feel like abject disappointments.

Over the years, many organizations have fallen into the trap of judging overall quality and success by Alpha standards. Alpha companies were those that were constantly scaling, expanding into new markets, and generating more and more value for shareholders. Those with simpler ambitions, that worked to become better at what they did best, procured a larger share of their current market, and generated dividends, were often deemed less successful.

In an Alpha world, most people feel like failures simply because they do not reach arbitrarily set goals or follow a traditional professional path. But there's no scarcity of reasons for not reaching the top. Bad luck can derail anyone. No one can control timing. (After all, an employee might be about to close a big sale when a massive snowstorm hits, so he misses the company's sales target.) Every organization has its share of politics, favoritism, and nepotism; the chairman may have had a favorite lieutenant who is seeking the same open senior vice-presidency as a deserving long-term manager. But the actual reasons for not "winning" don't matter terribly much in an Alpha company. No one wants to hear about them. *Close but no cigar* doesn't count in an Alpha environment.

In an Alpha culture where only a handful of stars earn accolades, big money, and special privileges, everyone else is treated as an afterthought. Remember: being good at what you do should provide you with satisfaction and fulfillment. But, in accordance with the Alpha logic, if that skill doesn't translate into reaching a top spot, it's practically worthless. Being part of the organizational network that actually makes things happen in a company is vital, but seldom appreciated and celebrated in an Alpha company.

Then as now, the majority of employees who work within the Alpha paradigm have felt undervalued and underappreciated. They feel their employers don't recognize their effort, hard work, skill, proficiency, or teamwork. Alpha companies rarely give individuals a chance or choice to find and focus on what they do best, but instead encourage them to keep ascending to the top—an environment that creates competition, envy, and rivalry within the ranks.

Is it any wonder so many people are unhappy at work? I meet unhappy employees from Alpha organizations every day of the week. "I need to talk to you about my career," They tell me. Most are ready to change jobs for a simple reason: They are not in the boss's favor or good graces. (Most work in corporate cultures where the Alpha boss hand-selects whom he wants to work on this or that project or initiative.) The CEO is neglecting them for plum assignments. He's leaving them out of key strategy meetings. I have counseled employees who are in favor with the boss, and those who are not, and the differences are profound. I once had lunch with a man we'll call "Mark," an anointed employee from a midsized company, who spent the first hour of our conversation telling me about his upcoming business trip to Australia, after which he planned to fly back to New York to help launch a pair of initiatives, the first with Amazon, the second with YouTube.

As he was talking, I remembered that there were four other employees at Mark's level. "Is everyone as insanely busy as you?" I said. Mark hesitated. "Not really," he said. The obvious conclusion: the other four employees at Mark's level were probably miserable. I knew the boss had chosen Mark as his designated go-to guy not because he was the smartest of the four, but because he had the best social skills. I considered asking him why he didn't bring George, his extremely intelligent but more reserved colleague, along with him to Australia. But would that really have addressed the core issue, namely, that no one in the company had ever spoken to George about his relational skills, or even asked him if he was interested in helping launch new territories abroad? No: it was far easier to send Mark, no questions asked. George didn't even stand a chance.

"How does your wife feel about all your traveling?" I asked. Mark told me that his work schedule was a sore point for his family. In fact, as a gesture of appreciation and apology, that week he had sent his wife to Paris on a small vacation. Despite being the boss's favorite, clearly it wasn't easy for Mark to be the company point guy. Which made it all the more baffling that no one had ever approached George, or the two other employees at that level, to make Mark's job a little easier.

Terry was equally frustrated. Since beginning his job at a well-known e-commerce company, he'd been doing a great job. But he was unhappy. Why? He didn't get the top slot. When we spoke, he still couldn't accept the fact that he'd been bypassed for the CEO job, and was actively looking for a new job at a new company. I might add that Terry's situation is common in hierarchical organizations. Employees figure out what is their silo, and whether they are stuck there, or on a fast track. The problem is, bosses almost never take the time to encourage them on ways to improve, or compliment them for the great job they are doing. Once upon a time, people could retire from an organization after thirty-five years of hard work, and feel proud of their contributions. But thanks to the cultural emphasis on getting ahead and climbing the corporate ladder—maybe even someday becoming a Master of the Universe—people who stay on in their jobs for years fear others will perceive them as failures.

Most organizations are top-down, with a rigid chain of command, and a formal, hierarchical structure. Not Beta companies. Which isn't to say Beta companies are necessarily informal. They are simply less rigid in their formality. They tend to organize in smaller, nimbler teams. Perhaps the best analogy is to today's armed forces, in contrast to the historical structure of the military. Today, countries fight wars much differently than they did only a few decades ago. There is still a commander who oversees operations, yet smaller armies are tasked with making judgments on the spot. In effect, everyone is a leader, and everyone is expected to carry out their jobs. Today West Point is teaching field officers how to make decisions in real time, to calibrate which decisions can't wait, and which ones should await the proper chain of command. Recently one young officer was told to accompany a few men to Afghanistan to scout for trouble, then return home with reconnaissance. As he made his way into the field, he encountered a large group of advancing rebels. Believing they were vulnerable, he organized his squadron to attack them, which they did. It was clear he had violated the chain of command. Yet when he later described to his superiors how he had weighed the decision, and considered the possible options, rather than facing a reprimand they hailed him as a hero. Would he still have been considered a hero if he had lost men during the mission? Yes. He had used his skill and his judgment in a real-time situation, consulted his squad, altered his plan, and taken appropriate action, along the way breaking hierarchy for the best interests of his men.

The same is true for sports teams and symphony orchestras. Yes, there may very well be a headliner, or a soloist, or a star, yet most marquee names understand that unless the words are on the page, and the music is in sync, and the costume and the dresser and the supporting players are doing what they are supposed to do, the performance will fall apart.

Not long ago, I went to see the musical *The Lion King* on Broadway, where I found myself seated beside a woman who was quietly taking notes during the two-hour-long performance. At intermission, I leaned over. "I'm just curious," I said. "May I ask what you're doing?" It turned out she was a Disney employee, from Quality Control, who showed up regularly at *Lion King* performances. Her goal was to ensure that the quality of the show remained as fresh and dynamic as it did opening night. If a cast member flubbed his lines, or a costume looked tattered, or the musicians came in late, these observations would show up in the feedback she gave to the show's producer and director, who then took matters up with the show's cast and crew.

Providing an opportunity for people to feel esteemed and self-actualized at work isn't an exercise in philanthropy. It actually provides companies with real-world practical benefits. When employees, and particularly managers, recognize that a company is giving them the chance to be their best selves, they develop a powerful emotional tie to the organization and to its leaders. When someone or something gives you a chance for true fulfillment, you respond with more than just gratitude. Employees who feel an emotional bond with a company are irreplaceable assets.

It's easy to spot the signs when employees lack emotional commitment to the organization:

- People grumble about the hours they're putting in;
- Turnover is high, particularly among young top achievers;
- Recruitment is difficult; there's little innovation or creative thinking; and
- There's more politicking than there is actual dialogue.

It's just as easy to spot the signs when employees *have* an emotional commitment to the organization:

- People give extra effort voluntarily;
- There's never a shortage of job candidates;
- Employees make personal and professional sacrifices to stay rather than leave;
- People feel free to think outside the box; and
- Meetings often result in lively debates.

As Stan Slap writes in his book, *Bury My Heart at Conference Room B: The Unbeatable Impact of Truly Committed Managers*, "A manager's emotional commitment is the ultimate trigger for their discretionary effort, worth more than financial, intellectual and physical commitment combined. It's the kind of commitment that solves unsolvable problems, creates energy when all energy has been expended, and ignites emotional commitment in others, such as employees, teams, and customers."[5]

Fred Smith, founder and CEO of FedEx, would agree. He's been quoted as saying, "When people are placed first they will provide the highest possible service and profits will follow."[6] FedEx's "people priority" is predicated on the company's strong belief that employee satisfaction and empowerment create an environment that encourages risk-taking and innovation in pursuit of improved service, which inevitably leads to increased profits. It's summed up best in FedEx's philosophical shorthand: "People—Service—Profit."

Not surprisingly, the Rochester, New York–based Wegmans supermarket chain, which we visited earlier, maintains a similar belief system. The Wegmans philosophy? "Employees first, customers second. We believe we can achieve our goals only if we fulfill the needs of our people."

Inherently unable to help employees meet their higher-level needs, Alpha organizations and leaders have to rely on rewards and punishments that focus exclusively on the most elemental human needs. Make no mistake: Money and a great office are always great and for a long time were adequate rewards for generations of Industrial Age algorithmic workers. But they can't compare to the incentives that today's Information Age heuristic workers demand. People today want the chance to be creative, the freedom to pursue their interests, and the opportunity to learn more and apply it.

Encouraging creativity is vital. Teresa Amabile of the Entrepreneurial Management Unit at Harvard Business School is one of only a handful of business academics who has studied the topic of creativity. Amabile's studies have found that in Information Age organizations, creativity isn't just a good idea; it's essential. Financial staffers have just as much incentive to think outside the box as marketing people. What hinders creativity? Internal competition and time pressures. What fosters it? Collaboration and freedom from distraction. Not surprisingly, happy employees are far more creative than fearful employees. And the intrinsic rewards of a job—making a difference, doing work that you enjoy—in many ways matter more than extrinsic rewards, such as money and position. Among other things, creativity encompasses the willingness to take chances. But when employees believe that everything they do has a direct impact on their compensation, more often than not they become distinctly risk-averse.

Look at Herman Miller: The innovative design firm claims that curiosity and exploration are among its two greatest strengths. To ensure those characteristics aren't lost, the company strives to respect and encourage risk—and practice forgiveness. "You can't be curious and infallible" is a company-wide motto. An employee who never makes mistakes, Herman Miller believes, may be an employee who isn't exploring new ideas.

Would design giant IDEO be the industry leader it were without a similar emphasis on risk-taking? I doubt it. No matter what IDEO is doing—collaborating with a smartphone manufacturer who wants to reinvent the gaming experience, or a government looking for ways to increase healthy eating in children or a hospital trying to improve its overall patient care—IDEO assembles a collaborative team made up of a broad range of industry experts. On one project, IDEO might assemble a business designer, a psychologist, a marketer, and a team of social scientists. On another, the company might bring together a team of industrial designers and engineers. The result: new companies, business models, brands, products, services, spaces, and interactive experiences that over the years have been behind everything from Apple's first computer mouse to Crest's stand-up toothpaste tube to the redesign of the economy class section of Air New Zealand's planes to the Palm V handheld device. IDEO CEO Tim Brown has been quoted as saying that an increasing number of global companies realize that innovation is a practical, scalable way of doing business, which is why IDEO has made innovation one of its core competencies.

By offering employees opportunities to attain their needs for esteem and self-actualization, Beta organizations typically end up with a workforce that is emotionally committed to the company.

Those are the kinds of people needed for the company to be all it can be as well. And Beta organizations, with their emphasis on the intrinsic rewards that lead to self-actualization, foster precisely the kind of environment needed to maximize creativity, a key element for business success in today's world.

The core elements of Beta—communication, collaboration, and curation—not only address the needs of Information Age organizations, but they also help today's knowledge workers achieve their highest individual needs. The good news: Beta works for both companies and people. Even better, adopting a Beta approach isn't difficult. But it *does* require adopting some new corporate attitudes and implementing some brand-new personal behaviors.

SEVEN

ELIMINATING ELITISM

Incestuous, homogeneous fiefdoms of self-proclaimed
expertise are always rank-closing and mutually
self-defending, above all else.

—GLENN GREENWALD

No two organizations are the same. Which is why no step-by-step template exists either for transforming an Alpha organization into a Beta company or for creating a new Beta business from scratch. Over the decades I've consulted with organizations, I've learned that each template faces unprecedented challenges and offers one-of-a-kind opportunities. Every situation is different. Every situation brings with it its own cast of characters. Having said that, a single core principle underlies every effort to create a Beta culture: Elitism must be eliminated.

Alpha organizations are by their very nature elitist. In fact, the Alpha concept is predicated on the notion that one person, or several individuals, happens to be better than everyone else in the organization. In turn, Alphas believe and preach that they stand atop the hierarchy as a result of their heightened intelligence, education, and creativity. As they see it, their authority stems not just from the rank or position they hold, but also from their overall qualitative superiority. Theoretically, people take their orders from Alpha leaders not out of respect for their position or rank, but in acknowl-edgement of his or her being better at whatever the organization values. The philosophical division of an organization into "the elite" and "the common" has a practical impact on every aspect of the company, from its culture to its physical environment.

By definition, elitism means simply, "the best." Now, I'm sure most of us faced with a serious medical condition would hunt down the "best" physician in the field, and that we would also encourage our children or grandchildren to apply to the "best" college they stood a chance of getting into. But in this case, when I use the word *elitist,* I am referring to organizations that talk a very good game about diversity, and emphasize the word in their promotional pam-phlets, and on their Web sites, but in fact, have next to none at all.

I once consulted for a well-known cosmetics company that was looking for a skilled digital practitioner to help evolve its online business in consumer goods. First, some context: Many cosmetics companies practice what I call "reverse diversity." It's an over-whelmingly female industry. Beauty companies may claim they are looking for the best employees with high-level credentials and the highest possible level of expertise, but in the end, those "best employees" better be women! I understood the company wasn't looking for a guy in a glue-spattered *Warcraft* T-shirt whose pants ended midcalf. I also understood that among her other job responsibilities, the ideal candidate would need to be able to con-vey her technological know-how in an easy-to-understand way to other female division heads. What's more, every woman who worked there looked more or less identical. Perfectly coiffed hair. Impeccable designer-label suits. Expensive shoes. The whole package.

In short order, I found a fantastic prospect, a woman. She was extremely smart. She could also explain the intricacies of technol-ogy to others simply and clearly. There was only one problem: Like many up-and-coming technology workers, she paid little attention to her appearance. Instead of browsing the flash sales on Gilt or ideeli, her passions lay in creating code and exploring new technology. The company's human resources director took one look at her and told me flatly, "The culture will reject her." In fact, the HR director went on, my candidate wouldn't even reach a point where the existing culture would even have the *opportunity* to reject her. Her new colleagues would dismiss her by her appearance at first glance.

I wasn't happy hearing this, but I also understood the rules of this particular workplace. My candidate *was* different (which was one of the things I liked about her), and the place *was* swarming with Alpha females. But the bottom line was she lacked a certain je ne sais quoi quality that the business world calls "executive presence."

So I did something I have never done before, or since. I took my candidate aside. "Look," I said. "I want you to go into this culture with your eyes open. Take a look around you. If you end up working for this company, you will serve as the leader of this digital initiative. You will be responsible for bringing in a team, and you and the team both have to mesh with the existing culture. The issue here is, people who work in company headquarters tend to look and act in a certain way." What I was trying to say, I went on, is that I couldn't just give her a desk, a chair, and a stylish coffee machine, and call it a day. Would she be willing to undergo a fashion makeover, with the company footing the bill?

Reluctantly but gamely—because she knew I was right—she agreed. A week later, she had a chic new haircut, her makeup was professionally done, and she was wearing a crisp new outfit. We both knew she was the same person as she was before, but with a difference: She was now empowered by her desire to compete, and by the knowledge that to make a difference in the company culture, first she had to embody and *live* the culture. Once she was hired, the company was altogether willing to accept the new changes and initiatives she was proposing, in order to scale the company. The company ended up hiring her, and she worked there successfully for many years. And over time, senior management began to grasp that a big chunk of their future resided in knowledge workers precisely like her—and that the information economy demanded that the company began hiring unconventional workers, whether it was guys with earrings, or women preoccupied 24/7 with coding.

In order to build a high-impact team, you have to teach executives that they are hiring people, not résumés. Eager to see in bold print a handful of "branded," big-name colleges and universities, a huge number of companies make the mistake of hiring the latter. They use people's academic credentials as reflections of their character, initiative, flexibility, and entrepreneurship. One private equity firm I consult with cherry-picks candidates exclusively from the senior classes of a handful of Ivy League colleges. An obvious point: most of the first-generation founders of these companies did not attend these schools, and certainly many would have been denied admission. What ultimately made these entrepreneurial founders so successful was their ambition and hunger for success. Once they attained it, they proceeded to *send* their children to these colleges and universities, and many firms today are hiring *that* generation of young people, based solely on their academic credentials as opposed to their characters.

Earlier, I used an orchestra conductor as a metaphor for the successful Beta leader. The conductor is not the general, or the majordomo, but instead, the creative director. He brings his players together onstage to carry out a common mission. The horns know it, the drums know it, the wind section knows it. In contrast, the culture of Alpha hierarchies is embedded in a chain of command, which doesn't necessarily tap into the complete brain trust, or the diversity that could help their organizations thrive.

I am not arguing against brand-name colleges and universities. Many extraordinarily smart, capable people graduate from them every year. But in today's enviroment, companies can't always hire people into titles. They need to hire them into their expertise. In turn, those people need to bring a sufficiently managed ego, and an innate flexibility, in order to fulfill multiple roles as the circumstances demand.

I wish I could say that elitism is a thing of the past, but it's not. Because it is the engrained path to the top, I constantly find myself challenging people about "titling"—the notion that unless you bear the name "Senior VP," chances are no one will perceive you as the "Senior VP." I recently spoke with the former female CEO of a small public company who, before that, was an extremely capable VP of international marketing. Her one goal in life was to become a CEO again. My advice to her was that she inform whoever was recruiting her that life is not all about being CEO. It's about being on a high-impact team where employees can make a difference. Instead of gunning for a title, I said, she should consider joining a company that's on a terrific growth trajectory. "So maybe you're not number one, but you're actually number three, or four," I said. "How would that sit with you?"

Obviously, this woman is not atypical. If a person has her eyes on the CEO slot, and is promoted instead to president, it's a *demotion* only if that person perceives it as one. To the candidates I counsel I like to say: If this job is a good role for you, if it fits your skill set, if it allows you to lead and make a difference in the community, then you've won. The only problem is, you just don't know it yet!

A huge success story, as well as a cautionary tale, Jill Barad began working as a product manager at Mattel back in 1981. Promoted to lead the company's "Barbie" line two years later, and tasked to transform the iconic doll into a series of new "roles" that would ensure her relevance for young girls coming of age in the 1980s, Barad was instrumental in Mattel's turnaround from near-bankruptcy into a newly strengthened industry leader. By selling Barbie as a shopper, a beachgoer, and a teenaged girl going on a date, Barad helped transform Barbie from a $200 million product into a $1.9 billion colossus.

By the end of the '80s, Barad had become an executive vice-president at Mattel. Still, she felt she wasn't progressing upward fast enough. So she issued an ultimatum: Unless then-CEO John Amerman made her a co-president of Mattel, USA, Barad would leave the company. He did, and she stayed. A few years later, Barad asked for assurance that she would eventually succeed Amerman as Mattel's CEO. Amerman agreed, and in the interim, named Barad chief operating officer and company president.

In the mid-'90s, Jill Barad reinvented Barbie again, this time around as a professional role model for young girls. Under the tag line "We Girls Can Do Anything," the new line of Barbies gave girls the implicit go-ahead to succeed in the real world. Barbie could be a physician, a teacher, or (like Barad) a wildly successful business-woman. Two years later, when John Amerman retired, Jill Barad became the new Mattel CEO, one of only four females in history to head up a Fortune 500 company.

Things went well at first. Barad was the brains and tactician behind a number of mergers that increased the company's bottom line, including alliances with the Pleasant Company, the creators of the American Girl Doll; Intel, the computer chip manufacturer; and Disney, which licensed Mattel to manufacture and market toys based on characters in Disney films. Barad expanded Mattel's global reach into new international markets. She joined the corporate boards of Microsoft and Reebok. She instituted flextime and half-day Fridays. Still, she had few allies within the company. Many found her too hard-edged, and not enough of a team player. During her tenure as CEO, numerous high-up Mattel executives resigned from the company.

The bigger problem? No one had ever really prepared Jill Barad for the CEO position. No one had ever counseled her about what, developmentally, she had to do in order to succeed, or the best ways to deal with colleagues, or a corporate board. Barad was among the most talented marketers in the business, but these skills did not always translate into managing people, reaching and sustaining financial targets, or strategizing for the future. The competition to reach the top alienated many of her colleagues. When Barad led Mattel to acquire software developer The Learning Company in 1999, a decision that ended up losing the toy company around $50 million, she ended up resigning as CEO under pressure from shareholders and investors, though it should be pointed out that Barad's brilliant marketing initiatives on behalf of Barbie and other divisions have since then gone on to increase Mattel's bottom line significantly. The bottom line was that this brilliant, trailblazing woman was an extraordinary vice-president of marketing, and would have continued to be an outstanding leader at Mattel if only the system had enabled her and her peer group to evolve together as a leadership *team*. But in this case, the hierarchical culture permitted only one winner.

Which begs the question: Should employees be trained for the next job up, and the next job after that? In some cases, the answer is yes, but in just as many instances, I know many people who love what they are doing, and simply want *more* of it: more work, more respect, more experience, more remuneration, and more opportunities to show they can finesse anything that comes their way.

Which brings us back to the problem of elitism. If the elite knows best, then what's the point of communicating with those employees on the front line? In general, Alphas might communicate with their people as a morale boost, just as a king strolls through his army's campground prior to a battle. *I'll inspire the "little people" with my presence.* Alternately, Alphas may communicate with their people to enhance their ego or image, like those CEOs who give me a tour of their offices and introduce to me staffers whose names they clearly cannot remember. *Look how close I am to my people— and how much they love me.*

If the elite are smarter than everyone, is there really any point in collaborating with the staff, customers, or competitors? Again, Alphas may occasionally solicit input as a public relations effort. For example, company-wide videoconferences might be installed in an attempt to provide staffers with an opportunity to offer ideas. Customers might be given e-mail addresses, or phone lines to call with comments. They might even be invited to participate in focus groups. In general, however, Alpha companies feel they have no need for authentic collaboration—and that all the answers reside with the leader. But in today's data-driven corporate cultures, there is no single answer. Data changes everything, today's companies must consider multiple analytic points, and winning strategies come from *everywhere* in the organization.

Careers in elitist organizations are about the acquisition of power and status, not the acquisition of knowledge and satisfaction. If the elite pursued a particular (and successful) path to the top, why, they must wonder, would anyone else need to follow another path? A leadership group of marketers sees no need for, say, engineers to be given the option to follow a complementary or alternative path. And since Alpha elites tend to define their status by their position in the hierarchy, most believe a career path should lead to a single destination: the corner office.

When an elite minority leads an organization, compensation is heavily weighted toward those in this select group—the "inner circle." Which is not to suggest that greater responsibilities do not merit increased compensation. But the ratio of senior executive to employee pay is now at historic levels, with U.S. CEOs in 2005 making 262 times the income of front-line employees, up from 71 times more in 1990, and 35 times more in 1980. It can be a challenge to inspire the troops with talk of teamwork when you earn more in a single day than most of your employees take home in a year.

Elitism isn't just an attitude; it is also reflected in how Alpha organizations organize their office and buildings. Separate floors for executives, with a protective moat of assistants keeping subordinates at bay, are commonplace in traditional companies. Executive cafeterias where the elite can eat without having to break bread with anyone else in the company; special parking lots where a gleaming Audi doesn't need to park next to a well-intentioned Toyota Prius; and executive perks like first-class travel and club memberships serve as visible reminders that an Alpha organization is the corporate equivalent of the haves and the have-nots.

"I've learned that symbols matter," Jon Miller confesses. "When I first took over at AOL, someone suggested I move my office. The company's top executives were all located on the fifth floor and it was like there was a moat around us. At the time I had so much else to do that I just didn't give the move priority. But looking back I wish I did. When you have a symbol of an imperial palace you create an 'us versus them' feeling inside the organization. Breaking that in a very visible manner would have helped me to get those in the organization better focused on externals. If you're worried about the guy next to you, you aren't worried about your competitor."

All of this elitism sends a message to those who aren't one of the select few: *You don't matter.* Might I add that this is the worst possible message to convey in the Information Age, when front-line employees in fact matter more than they ever have before? Product and service iterations today are constant, and in some industries— online gaming, for one—they are instantaneous. The front-line salesperson and the programmer writing code can have a far greater impact on their organizations' day-to-day bottom line than a senior-level executive in finance. Beta companies understand this, which is one reason why they seek to create cultures and environments that eliminate the "us versus them" dichotomy wherever it exists.

Transforming the physical manifestations of elitism isn't difficult, though it does require a deliberate effort by the team. John Morgridge, the former CEO and chairman of Cisco Systems, likes to tell the story of how once, when he touched down at an airport in a major city, he was greeted by a man holding a small posterboard with his name on it. It wasn't a limo driver. It was a guy who'd come to hand Morgridge a rail card for use during his visit. The actions and behaviors of everyone in the company, Morgridge explains, go a long way toward defining an organization's cultural values; in this particular case, cost cutting. Cisco management made it clear to employees that upper management used the same means of transportation as everyone else. Eliminating exclusive executive cafeterias and having everyone eat together isn't all that difficult, and democratizing parking lots requires nothing more than hiring someone to paint over names or take down signs. Rearranging floor plans may take additional effort, but it's far easier than redrawing the org chart.

Banishing elitist elements in a company's culture can be difficult. A corporate anthropologist or a savvy consultant can conduct a careful audit and prescribe appropriate changes. Even without hiring an outside expert to diagnose and help cure organization elitism, every company can take three general steps toward becoming a Beta organization:

- Develop and support facilitators;
- Recognize and reward craftsmen; and
- Build a learning organization.

Alpha organizations and leaders typically focus on metrics to determine success and advancement before singling out those people who sold the most, generated the greatest profit, and produced the most product. Employees who land in the lowest range are terminated. And those in the middle—that is, the vast majority of employees whose contributions might include those that aren't easily quantified—are seldom acknowledged and celebrated.

But successful organizations need more than just top performers. The person who binds a team together is seldom if ever the highest achiever. Those who reap the largest rewards are the individuals with a tunnel-vision focus on hitting goals and targets. These people can be courageous, decisive, confident, competitive, and visionary. But they can also be reckless, temperamental, opinionated, and selfish.

Most people find it difficult to relate to superstars whose deeds are often so out of reach. And superstars often have an equally hard time collaborating with solid performers who form the backbone of most companies. Top performers in an organization are often hard-pressed to understand the difficulties experienced by those who have yet to achieve their potential, which is why great artists are almost never great teachers, and great athletes are almost never great coaches.

So where do you most often find the people who do the little things that keep an operation humming; who serve as the links between various departments, divisions, or cliques; who represent the collective conscience or culture of the entire company; and who can rise above individual egocentric interests and promote holistic "ecocentric" interests? Generally, they are among the vast group of employees that form your organization.

Some of these employees are high-potential and most are team players and valuable contributors. I call these people "facilitators." They range from the office manager who reminds the executive to wish the receptionist a happy birthday (and hunts down a bouquet for the executive to present to her) to the senior vice-president, whose magnanimity and communication skills keep management council meetings from descending into angry debates or vicious critique sessions. They are the people who together create the moral compass of the community.

In Alpha companies, employees who inspire everyone to pull in the same direction rarely earn organizational rewards or recognition. The nurturers, the peacemakers, the organizers—to a man or a woman they are generally undervalued and sold short (and not just because of an organization's obsession with metrics, either). Moreover, the facilitator role is more often than not a position played by women. In an Industrial Age society with its rigidly defined, gender-divided home and work roles, nurturing was encouraged in women and discouraged in men. Females also gravitated toward the facilitator's role because they had few other options. A woman might climb her way out of the secretarial pool to become an office manager, but she rarely had an opportunity to compete for a spot as department head. For generations, as we have seen, Alpha companies generally undervalued team-building activity, as well as the traits and values women contributed to the workplace. Few organizations emphasized the development of "soft skills," or focused on the importance of emotional intelligence.

In an Information Age, nurturing behavior and team-building are essential ingredients for any company or institution that seeks to maximize its potential. Facilitators build and maintain lines of communication across an organization. They frame issues in ways that both the high achievers and the average performers can understand. Not least, they are a company's most natural collaborators. Comfortable playing a supporting role in the company, and encouraging others to do the same, they are the employees best positioned to promote and take advantage of curated career paths. And they enable the success of the other teams.

Rob Cross is a former IBM and Andersen Consulting manager who today runs a consulting group known as the Network Round-table, which analyzes social networks across organizations. Cross believes that a hidden social graph exists in all companies. According to CNN, a few years ago, the former Lehman Brothers firm sent three hundred top-performing vice-presidents on a four-day leadership workshop. There, they underwent a corporate "social network analysis" to help everyone better understand the networks surrounding them, the goal being to increase both performance and financial success. Using a proprietary survey that Cross developed, managers were asked to name each person in the organization who consistently gave them relevant, trustworthy information, and to write down which collaborations yielded the best financial results. Cross then drew up a graphic that explored the unseen internal networks, both weak and strong, that strung together Lehman's web of connections. According to CNN, "Several types emerged, including 'connectors,' who had the most extensive direct ties, and 'brokers,' who had the most diverse networks and who were key to getting things done. Then there were the 'bottlenecks,' who—either because they were overworked or because they hoarded information— kept things from happening." The upshot? "All the employees were able to see if they were on the periphery of networks, or in the middle of them."[1] From that day forward, based on what they had learned from Cross's survey, Lehman leaders were able to create and leverage a stronger, more efficient social network.

Cross's research confirms that an entire galaxy of well-defined individuals exists within every organization. Some are superstars. Others are facilitators, those men and women who make things happen, and who bring others together around a common vision. In truth, they may not be the best executors of whatever function they happen to carry out, but they are faithful, widely respected culture-carriers who live and breathe the organization's philosophy. I might add, too, that many CEOs are also facilitators, meaning that they have good ideas they could otherwise not convey without creating constituencies-within-constituencies, or trespassing on others' toes, or dealing with fiefdoms and political intrigue.

You would think that if you were an employee with a good idea, you could simply bring it to a company and go from there. But in cultures where CEOs are facilitators, CEOs have to figure out how to take that idea—and the culture-influencer who came up with it—and make it happen without mandating it. (Otherwise, people would be doing it simply because the CEO said they should.) Thus, the CEO facilitates by saying, or implying, "I think that's a good idea. Why don't we invite so-and-so to lunch to discuss a possible collaboration?" Or, "I have some extra R & D money in my budget we could consider using." Whether it's a new idea, a new opportunity, or a new account that calls for a new expertise, "facilitating" from the top requires a lot of understanding of your people, and a company's social networks. Frankly, it's uncommon, in large part because employees tend to tailor an idea or solution to what history shows the CEO will like or sign off on, which is why "managing up" is so commonplace in Alpha-driven companies.

Beta organizations need to pay as much attention to facilitators as to achievers. Individuals who can create and sustain teams must be singled out, recruited, and developed, in the same way companies have historically highlighted their most elite achievers. Companies have to be able to spot and recruit future sales managers, not just future stellar salespeople. They need to achieve greater parity of rewards between the facilitators and the achievers. At every level of an organization, individuals skilled at bringing people together need to be offered viable paths to advancement and chances to be recognized and rewarded.

"Missions are accomplished by teams, not individuals," says Jon Miller. "You don't want people who are thinking, 'Where will I be in five or ten years?' Today you want people for whom the mission they're going to be tackling with a team is what excites them. They'll figure out the next step in their working life when the time comes. There's a presumption that there will be further missions for them to take on and other interesting teams for them to join once they achieve the first mission. If there aren't more interesting missions, these people will leave for someplace where they join other teams to take on other challenging missions. It's the job of a Beta manager to articulate these missions and help develop or reconfigure the teams to tackle them."

Among the least appreciated, most profound changes to come from businesses finding themselves in a fast-paced, technologically driven world is that decision-making has changed. Compare the time it takes to write a few new lines of programming code to how long it once took to make new tools and dies for industrial machinery. Today, offerings can be tweaked daily in response to changes in the market and in available technology. Thanks to these improvements, customers and clients now expect them, which, in turn, requires rapid decisions by staffers.

This runs counter to the Alpha drive to centralize decision-making in a command-and-control environment. To survive and thrive in the Information Age, businesses need to push decision-making power down to those who are actually on the front lines creating the product or offering the service. Today, engineers, designers, content creators, and sales staff have the greatest influence on the quality of the actual product or service. Even in Beta companies, executives need to retain strategic decision-making and goal-setting, but command and control over tactics need to be pushed down the ladder. Because operations-level people are now so essential for success, more than ever before they need to be empowered and to have their value recognized and their performance rewarded.

Under the Alpha paradigm, top rewards derived exclusively

from climbing out of the operational ranks and joining the executive world. Personal and professional development consisted less of being someone who does things than of becoming a manager of *people* who did things. Anyone with financial or professional ambition had to accept that in order to gain more recognition and earn more compensation, he or she had to move into the managerial ranks.

But in an environment where decision-making must take place at the operational level, it's foolish to strip operation ranks of the best and brightest, and propel them onto an executive path. It can also be counterproductive. "We had a great software architect who, in order to follow the established career development trajectory had to become a manager," recalls Daniel Hamburger, President and CEO of DeVry Inc., one of the largest publicly held higher-education organizations. "We promoted him to manager and he was terrible. So not only did we have an awful manager but we'd also lost a great software architect. We decided to instead create a new position of senior software architect for him, putting him on a status and compensation level commensurate with the management position, but letting him focus on what he does well."

Hamburger finds that the same thing happens when people climb rungs, not just shift from craft to management. Over the years, he's seen academic deans who are outstanding at what they do, but who lack the necessary skills to make the traditional advancement to campus presidents. "We had to find a track for them to follow as well. It has been driven into people that they have to become the boss, so it's important to do some coaching, show them it's okay if they follow another path, and then help them find that path."

Companies that want to thrive in today's world need to recognize and reward craftspeople. Along the way, they need to bring the operational and executive tracks closer into balance. From the time of recruitment until the day people leave an organization, they need to be able to proceed along separate, but as equal as possible, tracks. Chief engineers need to be equal in compensation and prestige to senior vice-presidents; head designers must feel as valued as directors of marketing.

"I tell people it's like college: you have to pick a major," says Jon Miller. "Decide what you are, and act accordingly. And the company has to have the flexibility to recognize different roles and reward them, probably decoupling compensation and roles to some extent. You see that first in sales, where the top salesperson may earn a higher straight salary than the sales manager. A good organization will provide two equivalent development paths in its culture." Fred Wilson notes that in venture-backed tech firms, it's common for senior managers to get most of their compensation in equity and to take lower salaries than many of their top employees.

"If incentive compensation occurs only at the top, it sends the wrong message," says Gerry Lopez. "Incentives need to go as deep as an organization can afford to make it. In my experience, it's easier to manage in environments like Starbucks and Pepsico where everyone got options, than in organizations where only the top people got incentives. When everyone is compensated on the same basis it creates a commonality of purpose." It's also important to understand that recognition can be as important as rewards. "Over the years I've observed that recognizing effort, sometimes just with praise, can put people on a high for weeks. A simple two-line e-mail from a CEO that says 'Nice job,' or 'I loved your idea,' can make a huge difference in how someone feels about the company and themselves."

Fred Wilson adds that younger employees are generally pretty sophisticated about compensation. "People today are willing to take less material compensation if they can work in an environment that is healthier for them, or if the organization is creating long-term value and they have a stake in it, or if the organization is contributing to society."

People need to be encouraged and coached to pursue what they do best; to keep doing what they enjoy and what brings them fulfillment, rather than give it up. Top executives needn't earn any more in salary or receive any more ego perquisites than top operations staff. They can receive compensation for their increased responsibility in larger stock options, for instance. In a Beta company, it's not unusual to find a CEO receiving a lower salary than a chief software engineer, while having a larger equity share.

When an organization develops and supports facilitators as well as achievers, and recognizes and rewards craftsmen in addition to managers, it's well on its way to creating a Beta culture. But there's one other general element that needs to be added to the mix to eliminate elitism: It must also become a learning organization.

One way the elitism of Alpha organizations shows itself is in its competitive approach to human resources. Rather than viewing it as an ongoing resource, leaders often perceive human capital as something either to be stolen away from competitors or a potential problem to be eliminated. A great deal of effort is typically made to recruit talented people, and management expends considerable resources to ensure that when they hire, manage, or fire those individuals, the company is complying with legal requirements.

Beta companies recognize that inadequate resources are devoted to the development and retention of individuals. Alpha companies increasingly find that other Alpha companies are poaching their most important contributors. In turn, this battlefield has created an ongoing "war for talent" for skilled knowledge workers. Instead of trying to win in this constant tit-for-tat personnel raiding, Beta organizations develop strategic plans for human capital management that involve more than just hiring and firing.

Since existing human resources executives and teams are often too mired in compliance to take on what was viewed as a more creative role, many Beta organizations create new C-level positions with support staff to develop, implement, and manage these new strategic plans. Whether they're called Chief Talent Officer, Chief Learning Officer, Chief Retention Officer, or Chief People Officer, these individuals are tasked with building and maintaining learning organizations. In the same way that Beta leaders become curators of the ideas and creativity of their organization, Beta companies need to become curators of the professional development of their human capital.

Ernst & Young, for example, states that one of its core promises is to provide its people "with the right challenging and rewarding experiences, learning and ongoing coaching they need, to help them grow and expand their aspirations." And that goes for "whether it's an assignment in a new service line, office or country they aspire to work in." Ernst & Young sees its role as helping its people match their personal and professional goals to the company's clients' needs.

Pitney Bowes has an education program they affectionately call Pitney Bowes University. Consisting of paid college tuition and free online courses, it has enabled employees to rise from assembly-line worker to engineer and from office clerk to manager. The company's continuing education component encourages managers to expand beyond their current areas of expertise. The result? Increased motivation, engagement, loyalty, and productivity.

The Container Store, the Coppell, Texas–based storage retail chain, places a priority on recruiting high-caliber people and keeping them engaged. Its Continuing Education program brings employees from around the country and from every division of the organization to the headquarters for a three-day intensive course. Each department within the company gives a presentation describing its function, providing opportunities for creative career shifting as well as advancement. The course closes with a four-hour shift working in the neighboring distribution center, adding an *Undercover Boss*–like opportunity for bonding and empathy.

Beta organizations need to adapt this kind of educational role to retain good people. Just as employers took on the role of providing health insurance to boost recruitment and retention after World War II, so in upcoming years, employers will be increasingly providing employees with educational opportunities, with the military serving as a perfect example. In the future, individuals will enter an organization in part because they know it will provide them with college and post-college courses, and maybe even a degree. Yes, some of those people will put in their time, get their degree, and move on. But grateful for the education and the opportunity to perhaps further their learning, most will reenlist with the company. Today, education is so costly and so highly valued that providing it is inherently attention-grabbing—even more so in an era when people are hesitant to take on personal debt and reluctant to leave secure positions.

Beta companies that can give their people a chance to customize their professional development will benefit on numerous levels. First, the organization will be better able to recruit employees who are seeking learning organizations. Second, the company will be populated by people who are moving toward fulfilling their ultimate professional potential, making them the most valuable employees they can possibly be. Finally, as a result of providing both material and nonmaterial opportunities, the company will be better able to retain these high performers since employees will be that much happier in their work.

If you're searching for companies that will succeed now and in the future of the Information Age, they're easy to spot. Each will have its own unique solutions and approaches. But they'll all share three characteristics. Look for companies that are developing and supporting facilitators; that recognize and reward craftsmen; and that are tranforming themselves into learning organizations. In other words, look for Beta companies.

EIGHT

MANAGING EGO

> Sure I am a religious man who is also passionate about
> conserving the environment. But I am also a CEO, with all the bad
> habits and attitudes that are natural to the species. . . . I am still
> naturally self-interested, overconfident, full of pride, and eager
> to control a meeting as any CEO in America.
> Every day, I struggle with my ego.
>
> —TOM CHAPPELL, *Managing Upside Down*

The gap between knowledge and action often stretches into a gulf. That's because determining what you should do, or need to do, is a rational act. But actually transforming that knowledge into action, well, that often requires overcoming emotional and psychological hurdles. It's one thing for leaders to accept that their company needs to eliminate elitism by developing and supporting facilitators, recognizing and rewarding craftsmen, and becoming learning organizations. It's still another for leaders to set aside long-held Alpha beliefs and behaviors and step up to Beta leadership. Among other things, Beta leadership requires the conscious, careful management of a core component of the leader's psyche that enabled her or him to get to the top in the Alpha world in the first place, namely *ego*. It also requires creating a corporate culture that offers productive ways for individuals to exercise and satisfy their own egos.

The simplest definition of ego? Our self-image. It is the perception you and I have of who we are. In English we use the term *ego,* Latin for "I myself," to replace *Das Ich,* the German phrase originally used by Sigmund Freud, the Austrian psychoanalyst and neurologist, and which can literally be translated as "The I."

An individual who views himself realistically, and recognizes he has both strengths and weaknesses, has what we generally perceive to be a healthy ego. In contrast, an individual who is unable to see himself clearly, and who does not acknowledge that he possesses both strengths and weakneses, has an unhealthy ego. A person's ego typically leads him or her to preserve whatever self-judgment has already been made, compared to an individual with a healthy ego, who will hear a suggestion from a peer and weigh its merits objectively (since neither individual perceives himself as perfect). A person with an unhealthy ego will perceive that same suggestion as an unwarranted attack if he feels he's flawless or, conversely, if he feels he's worthless, as proof of his peer's own incompetence. Human beings are instinctively attracted to others who reinforce their ego-driven self-judgments. They automatically gravitate toward people who treat them the way they feel they deserve to be treated, and avoid those who treat them in ways antithetical to their self-image.

To survive and thrive today and into the future, business leaders need the appropriate self-awareness to *manage* their egos. Beta leaders need to be fully invested in the present, rather than viewing situations and individuals through the lens of the self or focusing on future moves on the corporate chessboard. As Tina Sharkey, a well-respected consumer executive and former chairman and global president of BabyCenter, has said, "Companies have to stop being 'egosystems' and instead become ecosystems." To this end, Beta leaders must take a moment to question why they respond the way they do to a suggestion. Do they have a bias or a personal issue that colors and slants their judgment, or are they coming from a place of experience and wisdom? Are they considering the unintended consequences of decisions and actions? Far from being perceived as indecisive, this kind of introspection rightly comes across as respectful of divergent points of view—a trait that today's employees cherish in their leaders, and that contributes to an organization's long-term success. And that is one of the core characteristics of a managed ego.

By their very nature, egoSystems are defined by bias and control. When a leader says, "I think we should hire this guy," isn't he really saying that he likes the candidate, can foresee working alongside him, believes his new employee will follow his directions while offering little to no resistance—and that no one in the organization can fault his leadership for deciding to hire the guy? Nor will the leader have to share his candidate with anyone else in the company. His new hire will be a loyalist—*his* loyalist. That's the egoSystem talking.

Now, what if a leader finds himself faced with a hiring decision involving a second candidate who is equally qualified, yet far more of a maverick than the first? This second candidate has big, possibly disruptive ideas. He is naturally assertive, and comes from a culture that encouraged free-form ideas, where employees were given permission to communicate whatever was on their minds. Frankly, our leader is slightly afraid of the second candidate! Collaborating with him would require more work, more effort, more dialogue. The thing is, the second candidate has better, more compelling ideas than the first candidate.

That's the quandary: In an egoSystem, almost by default, the leader will hire the candidate he can control. But in an ecoSystem, the leader knows full well that the most outstanding cultures often result from disparate personalities exchanging wildly diverse ideas. He is genuinely exhilarated by the prospect of taking on a new hire who might challenge and negotiate the path along the way to uncovering some groundbreaking new ideas and initiatives.

Let's take another example. A corporation may find itself faced with two competing directions, or opportunities, it could explore. A CEO's team might tell him that rather than buying a new company outright, the organization should consider a joint venture. Sure, a joint venture would be messier in terms of the two cultures integrating and meshing, but at the same time, the two companies could join forces with less risk than if the corporation went out and bought the second company. In an egoSystem, a CEO's tendency might be not to think twice: he will acquire the other business. Unconsciously he may be telling himself, *Who cares? Right now it makes sense, and also grows my revenue. Chances are I'm here only for the next five years, anyway. I may get fired, anyway. At least I'll be remembered as someone who got credit for an acquisition, even if it ultimately goes awry, and I'll still get a bonus at the end of the year.*

In an ecoSystem, consciously or unconsciously, the CEO's internal monologue might instead go like this: *You know what? If I have to build this new Boeing, and I carry out a joint venture with a parts manufacturer, I can still spread the risk by using three different suppliers.*

This example is hypothetical. But in an egoSystem, there would be little doubt or indecision. The CEO would snap up the company and expand his fiefdom. In an ecoSystem, the CEO would consciously try to understand how to build a collaborative universe around the opportunities before him. Based on my past experience, the ego—and not the eco—tends to make most decisions. It emphasizes the *I* rather than the *We*. Here, as always, I can't help but come back to the crucial importance of self-awareness in a business setting. People have to understand who they are and why they make the decisions they do. Is it because it suits them and is safely within their comfort zone, or is it for the greater good of the company and the people? I often tell people I counsel, "Change is not good or bad. If we could convince ourselves that change is always good, quite frankly we would change every day. But we don't, because we fear the unknown. And it is easier to stay where we are, than to take risks." To change an egoSystem into an ecoSystem, I counsel CEOs to explore all possible intended and unintended consequences. I recommend that they talk to their kitchen cabinet, then make a decision that has a built-in safety net. That way, if something goes wrong, it is not about the CEO. It is instead about the data, and about the team, and about the leader having made the very best decision on behalf of the entire *organization*.

The old adage that great leaders need to hire people smarter than themselves is hyperbole. The reality is that successful Beta leaders need to be self-aware enough to recognize the gaps in their own skill sets, and confident enough to hire intellectual equals who can then fill those gaps. A great strategic CEO who knows she's a good, but not great, operational leader will find a great COO who provides that tactical skill set, just as an outstanding marketer who's not a top-flight financial executive will be on the lookout for a skilled numbers person.

Armed with a managed ego, the very best Beta leaders understand intuitively how to play to their strengths, and build the very best team possible around them. A core trait of the Beta model is the capacity to relinquish the need to control everything, and instead, bring in new people who share a company's cultural sensibility and can also augment the leader's skill set. As I noted in the example above, the best Beta CEOs are not in the habit of hiring their doppelgängers. Instead, they hire people with whom they are willing to partner. You might even dub this a distinguishing characteristic of a Beta organization. Throughout this book, I have likened a Beta organization to a great symphony or sports team. Both may have superstars on the stage or on the floor, but symphonies and winning teams also need people who know how to play together, who don't hog the ball, and who know how to pass and rebound.

When I'm called in to meet with young CEOs in start-up

organizations, the org charts they present me with are almost breath-taking in their focus and solipsism. Everyone and everything in the organization reports to those guys! At an early stage of a company's evolution, most twenty-something CEOs feel the need to control absolutely everything. The problem is, if they maintain that grip, they will never be able to grow and scale the company. At some point, I advise them that what they really need to focus on the most at this early stage isn't the cult of the CEO, but a professional organization of people who can do their jobs well; who share the CEO's goals, missions, and values; and to whom the CEO can delegate responsibilities. Which doesn't mean that the CEO should not have input, or that he or she is not ultimately steering the ship. It means only that the CEO cannot be on the bow with the wind whipping his face 24/7. Given the structure of most of today's businesses, when a CEO has so many external functions (dealing with the board, engaging in investor relations, serving as the company's public face), a leader needs to establish an environment where the natural sum-of-the-parts mentality is larger than what a single individual can provide.

Which brings me to what I call "Tribal Councils." A Tribal Council is exactly what it sounds like—a low-key gathering of twelve to fifteen people in an organization. My goal in setting up these get-togethers is to create a safe place, a refuge from the hierarchical dynamics of business-as-usual. Beforehand, I link up a company veteran with a more junior member of the team. Maybe I'll ask them both to read an article from the *Harvard Business Review* that explores how to bring a company's people together on a vision around a deal. Alternately, they can discuss a business development call both have made to the same client. Next, by bringing in their own experiences and war stories, we figure out how they can best summarize the paper. Typically, the senior employee will begin free-associating. He might recall a merger in which he played a role, why it succeeded or why it floundered. The junior employee might then chime in about how scared she was when asked to participate in *her* first merger.

Over the years I have witnessed some of the toughest Alpha veterans melt as they interact with more junior colleagues. Sure, they may be big shots now, but they can easily recall how it was when they were just starting out. And the younger employees, who are often overflowing with youthful self-confidence, grasp that their elders have skills and experiences that are worth learning about and emulating.

Before the Tribal Council begins, I remind everyone in the room that we are in a safe place devoted to learning. Nothing anyone says will be ridiculed, or seen as naïve. Our mission is to talk *with* each other, not at each other. We're there to share ideas, opinions, experience, triumphs, and mistakes.

Experience has taught me that Tribal Councils are among the most powerful tools there are for bringing people together, transforming learning into an interactive sport, and facilitating natural collaboration. As employees interact over everyday business issues, Tribal Councils gently shatter workplace barriers. They foster self-awareness and an awareness of others. They work so well, in fact, that when they're over, Tribal Elders typically ask their younger colleagues to accompany them on a sales call, in order to create a natural mentorship or sponsorship.

An apt corollary would be a book group, in which the host posts the book that the group will be reading that month. People show up, not necessarily always because they love the book, but because the book enables deeper conversation in a nonconfrontational, nonjudgmental way. Back in the days when I worked in private equity, I frequently led Tribal Councils to ensure that a company's teams were interacting with one another, and to remind organizations that they are all in this together.

In addition to having the self-awareness to manage their own egos, Beta leaders need to understand how their employees' egos influence attitudes and behaviors. It's a fact: People pursue behaviors that provide them with the best chances to gratify their egos. When an organization recognizes and rewards only individuals and their achievements, people tend to compete. In contrast, when an organization recognizes and rewards group achievements, people form teams and collaborate. Simply put, most people in organizations will behave in ways that provide them with the greatest ego gratification. If that means acting like Alphas, they'll act like Alphas. If it means behaving like Betas, they'll be team players. Obviously, this has compensation implications since money remains a large element in employee ego gratification. If financial rewards are limited to only a handful of individuals, or to a single winning team in the company, it will create a competitive environment. On the other hand, if compensation rewards are allowed to trickle down to others in the company, the organization will become more cohesive.

A good example is how Google reportedly linked the entire organization's compensation bonuses to the success of its social networking effort, Google+. According to *Business Insider,* CEO Larry Page sent out a company-wide memo to all his employees, letting them know that a quarter of their year-end bonuses were tied to the performance of the new social media initiative. Even employees who weren't directly responsible for the roll-out were enjoined to test it out and recommend it to their families and friends.[1]

While powerful, the lure of ego gratification is not always rational. In a paper for the journal *Personality and Social Psychology Bulletin,* psychologists Roy Baumeister and Liqing Zhang describe how "the motivation to maintain and enhance favorable views of self" can make people "more prone to become entrapped in losing endeavors." In their study, college students were given cash and allowed to use it to gamble on activities that were primarily stacked against their winning. Some students were subjected to veiled put-downs. Others were not. The students who had their egos threatened were more likely to gamble and lose more money. The study found that individuals commit more to a losing course of action when their ego involvement is higher. This study goes a long way toward explaining why some bankers continue to pour money into failing investments, if they were the ones who first made them; why fledgling entrepreneurs mortgage their homes to continue funding start-ups that aren't meeting projections; why executives will continue to push self-created initiatives that have no chance of success; and why the leaders of nations vow to stick out unwinnable wars.

Thanks in no small part to ego involvement created by years of success, numerous industries have continued to pursue losing paths, failed to note incoming technological revolutions or cultural trends, or refused to consider future scenarios that might affect their industries. At the onset of the dot-com era, many companies, including department stores and major newspapers, sold off their dot-com businesses in order to increase short-term revenue. Back then, these companies perceived Web sites as stand-alone entities that weren't integral to their industries as a whole.

Consider how the recording industry failed to foresee the digitalization of music, or that CDs retailing for $18.99 were beyond the budget of many adolescents who made up a core music demographic. Nor did the industry grasp that the younger generation wasn't especially loyal to the musicians they liked. Once they had heard an artist or singer, it was time to move on. They wanted something new.

It wasn't just the changing tastes of consumers that transformed the music industry; it was also new technology, file-sharing, and YouTube. Why spend money on a new CD if you could download individual songs online for $0.99 a pop, or use computer technology to record those songs from YouTube, and import them to your iTunes folder? Why buy a ninty-minute-long concert video when you could watch clips online? As for the artists, ask Justin Bieber how essential record companies are. Then as now the Internet permits everyone with varying degrees of talent to post their own songs and videos on the Web, thereby bypassing traditional industry gatekeepers. And by leveraging the power of televised talent competition, record producer and music-competition judge Simon Cowell (*American Idol* and *The X Factor*) proves it is possible to create a musical sensation, and a platform, simultaneously. Today, with major CD chains shuttering their doors, the CD has become charming but inessential, the victim of an industry that took its eyes off the road.

The recording industry is hardly alone. The Internet has helped demolish numerous industries. Did Blockbuster see Netflix up the road? In turn, did Netflix see Redbox coming? Did Redbox understand that, with more and more consumers using personal computers, the era where a family hunkered down in front of a television set was over, that most of us were perfectly happy to screen the latest episode of *Mad Men* or *The Office* on our laptops? Did the travel industry foresee that the legwork they once carried out for customers—booking flights, reserving no-smoking rooms in select hotels, arranging day trips, and arranging tickets to the very best tourist attractions—could be done with a mouse click?

The point is, ego involvement can seriously cripple an industry. Then again, to be a leader requires being somewhat of a narcissist. Because adjectives like *vain, conceited,* and *selfish* are used to describe narcissists, we tend to use the word pejoratively. But narcissism is really no more than thinking highly of oneself: in other words, having self-esteem. It takes narcissism to assert yourself and your ideas, to take on responsibilities, to think outside the box, and to seize opportunities. No one succeeds in an organization or profession without having *some* degree of narcissism.

But just as there are healthy and unhealthy egos, there is both healthy and unhealthy narcissism. The confident, assertive, optimistic traits of healthy narcissism can, if not tempered by empathy for others, turn into a pathological selfishness and self-focus. Unhealthy narcissists are arrogant and unable to feel ashamed. They have a sense of entitlement because they think themselves special and superior. They feel envious of others' success and have no compunction about exploiting people for their own aims. To an unhealthy narcissist, everyone else exists solely to meet his or her own needs. If the other person doesn't contribute to the narcissist's agenda, they become irrelevant.

Elitism can turn a leader's healthy narcissism into a destructive force. When rewards and information are distributed according to hierarchical position, it creates a culture of undue competition. Collaborative, communitarian, and communicative efforts, on the other hand, can turn inherent narcissism into a productive force. As I mentioned earlier in this book, I've seen CEOs who encourage their own divisions to compete inwardly for the spoils. They consider that internal competition drives teams to do their best. (I also once knew a hot-tempered investment banker who proudly told me he encouraged his own two under-ten sons to fight, that that was the way the world worked, and it was fantastic preparation for the workforce—and the world—they would someday be entering. Needless to say, he and I are not the closest friends!) Of course there is natural competition in the business world—Coke versus Pepsi, MasterCard versus Visa, Microsoft versus Apple—but from my perspective, when you create or concoct unnatural competition inside your own company, it creates an environment where you cannot learn anything new from anyone else—where you must do everything yourself. Which I consider *un*healthy.

By itself, narcissism is neither good nor bad. Most if not all entrepreneurs tilt toward narcissism; if a hard, healthy dose of narcissism didn't fuel their determination and ambition, most wouldn't have the courage, the passion, or the stick-with-it-ness to realize their ideas. It is more a matter of balance. Only when excessive ego threatens to derail a company, and a person stops listening to the people around him and becomes fixated on always being right all the time, to the extent of being unable to see the forest for the trees, does narcissism becomes a toxic force. And frankly, numerous CEOs fit this description! The danger comes when leaders feel that being right and winning are far more important than the organization becoming a place devoted to learning, evolving, and adapting new points of view.

The anthropologist and psychoanalyst Michael Maccoby has written about the corporate narcissism that ensues when a top executives turns his or her management team into a pack of supporters who enable his or her own narcissism, noting that the process is about "reproduced copies, not about originals." As a result, these Alpha-driven narcissists end up more committed to their own interests than to those of the organization or its constituents. "A certain kind of charismatic leader can run a financially successful company on thoroughly unhealthy principles for a time," Maccoby concedes, adding that eventually, inevitably, there will be problems.

Several years ago, I sat next to a vice-chairman of a hugely successful company who told me he was not going to put any money in social media. "You don't have to spend money on that stuff," he told me. "You just use your existing people and get them engaged. No one even looks at social media anyway." When my jaw had finished dropping, I told him that I had just spent nearly six months alongside the employees of one of the most famous newspapers in the country, teaching them how best to monitor their Twitter feed, and reminding them that they could uncover some of their best stories online. "It doesn't matter what you and I think," I told him politely, "because you are not a member of the digital generation. I don't tweet. You don't tweet. But the thing is, your grandchildren tweet, your employees tweet, and most important, your customers tweet." And if he didn't get on the ball, I told him, the marketplace would leave him and his business behind. By the time I left, he'd gotten the message loud and clear.

In a Beta environment, on the other hand, leaders can become what Maccoby calls "productive narcissists." Their self-esteem provides them with the confidence to do what they feel needs to be done, without the constraints of fear and insecurity. At the same time, their empathy and concern for others, and their ability to offer chances for others to gratify their egos, result in a powerful mix. The Beta leader's charisma and the opportunities he or she provides for others in the organization to achieve self-actualization are what create an organization poised to prosper in the twenty-first century.

There are few better examples of corporate narcissism becoming destructive than the history of the MS-DOS operating system. Back in the 1980s, IBM ruled the computer industry. The uniformity of opinion among the company's executives fostered the belief that hardware—IBM's strength at the time—mattered far more than software. So when the company set out to create a "personal computer," it paid scant attention to the operating system software that was the foundation of the machine. UVN approached Bill Gates of the then-small software company Microsoft in order to procure an operating system. The hardware guys who ran IBM saw nothing wrong with letting Gates and Microsoft retain the rights to the operating system, MS-DOS, as well as the ability to market it separately from their boxes. The eventual result was IBM's loss of the preeminent position in the personal computer industry to Microsoft.

Having risen to the top in Alpha environments, it's likely that successful individuals' natural narcissism has taken on potentially destructive tendencies. Executives need to shift their own and the company's focus from "me" to "us." They need to weave people together into teams, rather than set them against each other in competitions for power and status. They need to help individuals identify and develop core competencies, and put those people into situations where skills can be used to meet shared, company-wide goals. They need to ensure the organization recognizes and rewards the achievement of these shared goals so employees can get ego gratification from being collaborative Betas rather than competitive Alphas. Finally, they need to foster communication up and down the hierarchy, and across disciplines and divisions.

The Beta leader plays the prime role in establishing an organization's vision and explaining its mission, but he or she gives people freedom in determining how they tactically deploy to serve the mission. A Beta leader creates an environment in which good ideas flourish and people feel protected and valued; an organization in which people feel empowered. That provides them with the opportunity to gratify their own egos and keep narcissism from becoming disruptive.

"I've had the great fortune to work for a number of outstanding leaders over the years," recalls Gerry Lopez of AMC Theatres, "including Roger Enrico at Pepsi and Howard Schultz at Starbucks. They are two very different guys, but the common link is that they were both about achieving results through people, not strategy and tactics. They found the right people, put them in place, and let them do their thing. The great lesson was: it's about leading the people, not leading the business."

When Daniel Hamburger first became CEO of DeVry, he started stepping out of board meetings at various points so the directors could have an uninhibited conversation about his decisions or actions. "One day it hit me, why don't I do that at my leadership team meetings as well so they can feel less inhibited and become more empowered? I do that two or three times a year now and the feedback I've gotten has been very appreciative."

There is probably no better example of empowerment than Nordstrom. The upscale department store chain renowned for its customer service is also famous for having just one rule for employees: *Use good judgment in all situations.* Jim Nordstrom, of the third generation of the family to lead the firm, believes that too many company rules disempower employees, and that they start thinking—and acting—as though rules matter more than customers. Empowered employees are the key to Nordstrom's unparalleled customer service. And giving that kind of unparalleled service provides a good dose of ego gratification to the employees.

A metaphor for this kind of Beta organization is a monastery. Despite their self-awareness, the individual monks set aside disruptive narcissism so that they can play their role in the community and work for the common good. Although he is nominally in charge of the monastery, the abbot sets aside his own potentially disruptive narcissism by striving to create an environment in which ideas and feelings are shared, and in which everyone is seen as contributing to the community.

That kind of collaborative equality needn't be limited to the religious world. During his decade and a half at DuPont, Bill Gore was struck by the efficiency and dynamism of the organization's "task force teams": temporary interdisciplinary ad hoc groupings that operated outside the corporation's formal hierarchy to attack problems. When Gore formed his own company, he took that idea to the next level. His firm, W.L. Gore and Associates, is what Gore calls a "lattice" organization. The company has a flat structure and everyone has the same title: associate. There are no permanent chains of command or channels of communication. Leaders take the place of bosses, and associates choose which leaders to follow. Associates communicate directly and are accountable to each other. Teams form around projects or ideas, and grow or shrink organically. Gore's extreme Beta structure has resulted in the firm becoming a perennial member of *Fortune*'s Best Companies to Work For list. What's more, the concept has translated well. Its UK, German, Italian, French, and Swedish operations have all won similar accolades.

Companies need not take so extreme an approach as Gore to gain the advantages of a company-wide managed ego. The fundamental work unit at Whole Foods, for example, is the self-directed team, which has regular meetings to brainstorm and problem-solve, and encourage and recognize one another's efforts and accomplishments.

The best way for leaders to make an attitude and behavior shift, and prevent narcissism and egos from impeding their success, is to be as aware as possible of their own motives and feelings, and the needs and wants of others. To borrow a term from Buddhism, Beta leaders need to practice *mindfulness* and encourage peers and employees to do the same. That may sound simple; and it's not. Destructive narcissistic attitudes are usually irrational and unconsidered. And the behaviors that result from them are reflexive and unplanned. Brought out into the conscious mind, their irrationality and thoughtlessness become apparent and they're easier to ignore or overcome. By working as hard as they can to focus on what is happening at any one moment, what they are working on, whom they are speaking with, or the surroundings they are passing through, leaders can go a long way toward eliminating habitual, thoughtless, reflexive, and perhaps overly narcissistic actions.

Rather than acting or reacting reflexively, considering how you are or will be affected, take a moment first to consider how others might react to what you say, or respond to what you do. For instance, instead of firing off a quick e-mail, pause first, reread the note, and think about the wide variety of ways it could be received. Avoid drama and extreme behaviors. Eccentric, volatile behavior may be accepted in creative individuals and Alpha prima donnas, but it won't help build a Beta organization.

The very best Beta leaders I know act mindfully and humbly. How could they not when most of today's business koans revolve around service and bottom-up leadership? Self-effacing Beta leaders make it a point to place their companies before their own egos. They don't need a camera in their faces to validate their own leadership. I once worked alongside a Beta leader I'll call "Bill." Bill was not the CEO, but he was partnered with the CEO, who was by far the more public-oriented of the two men. The CEO was the guy who met with bankers, who articulated the company vision to the press and the public, who was proud and a little overeager to stand up before a group of people at this or that industry shindig. In contrast, Bill was the unofficial face of the organization, a warm, confident man with great people skills who could tell employees he knew times were tough but that everyone in the company was going to make it through in the end. The thing is, if you saw Bill across the room, you would never suspect how successful he was. For Bill, it wasn't about the money, the Ferrari, the country club membership, or the big house. He was simply doing what he loved, which was helping build great companies—and great employees.

Thanks to his focus on his own people, Bill helped me facilitate a "Lifeline Exercise," an initiative I bring to many companies that I counsel. It's simple: I ask employees to tell the stories of their lives, up to and including the schools they went to, the teachers who influenced them, the mentors who gave them a leg up, their victories *and* their setbacks. Why? Because most people who sit at desks only a few feet away from one another know practically nothing about their colleagues' lives, where they live, how many children they have, or how long their commute is every day. I've carried out the Lifeline Exercise with over one hundred companies, and the results are always revealing.

For example: In one company, there was an extremely able, but emotionally closed-down, manager. Yet when we did the Lifeline, he opened up. He told his colleagues that two years earlier, he was engaged to be married when he and his fiancée were involved in a car accident. His fiancée was killed; he'd escaped the crash with only a few injuries. From that moment on, his fellow employees embraced him in an entirely new way.

Which brings me to another point: Company-wide understanding is a major characteristic of Beta companies. You cannot separate who you are from who you are at work. Not only that, but once the Lifeline Exercise wraps up, employees are always hungry for more. Think about it: When we move into a new neighborhood, or community, we make it a point to get to know our neighbors. We want to meet their families. We want to find out if we share one another's values. One of the strengths of the Beta leader is the capacity to understand the commonalities shared by the people in the organization, and how to create a culture that encourages people to care about one another.

From my perspective, this Beta inclusiveness is contagious. More and more Alpha organizations are turning to Beta initiatives, such as building community housing or organizing company road races for a good cause. These companies, and their employees, are rightfully proud of these initiatives. After all, causes bring people together, and unite us around a single mission. Yes, it is good business to show your concern for the environment, or carry out your business in a socially responsible way, but at the end of the day, authentically advocating for good causes ties employees emotionally to a company. (Here, I emphasize the word *authentic,* since most employees can sniff out a bogus "socially responsible" corporate cause in a second.) Going forward, in an era where more and more young technology workers can write their own professional tickets, working for a socially conscious organization is a crucial component of why employees stay where they are. People don't stay in places where no one nurtures them, and where there's no community. They stay in places that make them look forward to coming into work every morning. And Beta leaders know that a crucial element of their own success comes from doing what is in the best interest of the community—which, coincidentally, creates an opportunity to be part of an extraordinary community, too.

My advice? Focus on your interpersonal skills. Ask trusted associates to point out any unconscious habitual mannerisms you might have, such as crossing your arms or gazing past people when you are talking to them, then develop techniques to break these bad habits. It's not enough to be a great public speaker and mass communicator. You need to connect with people on a one-to-one level. Maintaining eye contact, smiling, and asking questions shows empathy. That said, it's easy for people to adopt those mannerisms as a facade. Take the effort to heart to turn appearance into reality. Pay attention to the answers you receive and respond to them. Take a moment to really observe people and their surroundings. Remember that other people are complete human beings, not cardboard cutouts. Noticing an unusually crowded desk or a disheveled appearance could indicate extreme time pressure or an unusual workload. Verbal tics or unusual mannerisms could be signs of distraction or fear that you could work to alleviate.

Paying attention to the humanity of others and showing that you care for them as people will yield immeasurable benefits. One of my clients complained to me about what he bluntly thought was the weakness and lack of ambition of an executive he'd inherited when he took over a sales organization. I held a meeting with the leadership team. When I went around the room getting ideas and feedback, sure enough, this executive demonstrated relatively poor verbal skills. I closed the meeting, as I often do, by soliciting further input via e-mail. The next morning I received a brilliant and insightful e-mail from the "weak" executive. When we spoke, he could barely articulate his thoughts. But when he followed up later in the day with a second, highly astute e-mail, I realized he was an extremely bright individual who communicated much better in writing than verbally. All that was needed for this executive to shine and become a top contributor was to be given a chance to process and write down his ideas, rather than vocalize them.

The need to think about people humanely applies not only to individuals but to groups as well. I was called into another client's firm to help him solve a problem. His company had just completed a crash development project that had required the team to work almost 24/7 for two months. It was an enormous success. But a month later, two of the team members left their jobs to work for a competitor. *Why?* my client wanted to know. I asked him what the company had done to celebrate the launch. He looked at me, puzzled. *Nothing,* he said. His team simply resumed their normal working hours. Rather than acknowledging how working those insane hours had affected the team members and their families, the company turned its back on the human impact. It could have offered the team time off, or a bonus, or the chance to work at home one day a week for a month—*anything,* really, to show their appreciation and gratitude. Little wonder that when no thanks were forthcoming, some team members decided to bolt.

Beta leaders also need to work on creating a safe environment so that people can offer ideas and opinions freely. It's one thing to solicit suggestions. It's another to treat them with respect, whatever their merit. A Beta organization's goal should be to have a culture in which there are no "bad" ideas, just ideas that lead to other ideas.

While sitting in on a meeting at one of my clients a few years back, I saw how destructive an "unsafe" environment could be. The leadership team of this media company felt they weren't getting enough input from the company's younger associates. In response, they decided to solicit ideas through a series of meetings in which executives met with younger associates from various divisions and departments for brainstorming sessions. At the meeting I attended, a young man offered up a somewhat abstract idea about creating affinity groups for each of the company's brands. Granted, his presentation was rough, and his concept wasn't fully developed, but it took courage for him to speak up, and his thinking was, for that time, outside of the box. The executive running the meeting was superficially polite in response, yet her obviously condescending tone was picked up by all the other young people at the meeting, who proceeded to offer nothing but routine suggestions.

Beta leaders need to seek out feedback and ideas from multiple sources at every level of the organization, and from outside the organization. Work with human resources to build feedback systems and programs. Most important, be receptive to what you hear. Don't jump to conclusions about what the other party is saying and quickly counter. Instead, pay close attention to what's being said, and then repeat back to the speaker what you believe you heard them say. Apart from demonstrating respect for their feelings and ideas, this provides a chance for leaders to correct misunderstandings. Don't react defensively and fall into rationalizing. Encourage rather than discourage creative thinking. If that young man who suggested affinity groups was encouraged for his creativity, he might very well have eventually helped the firm pioneer the development of online communities and the use of social networking. Instead of being discouraged, he could have been given direction and development opportunities for his thinking.

It's vital for organizations to really work on this receptivity to new ideas and feedback. Daniel Hamburger believes that "getting people to say what they really think is almost against human nature. In our families and social situations we're taught not to tell people what we think if it could be construed as being critical in order to save their feelings. I think getting past that tendency is one of our biggest challenges." As part of that effort, Hamburger has been encouraging managers to do their own exit interviewing and not rely only on human resources. "When you do that, and also conduct employee surveys and solicit feedback, you uncover issues you didn't know you faced. Show that you listen, and then respond in some way, and people will feel more comfortable in speaking up."

Beta leaders need to cultivate humility. This doesn't mean giving up self-confidence. It means remembering that you're not perfect, and showing you're fully aware of that. Self-deprecating humor will improve your stature in others' eyes. It also means putting the company's collective needs above your own. Beta leaders make sure they're the first in the organization to give up compensation when times are bad, and the last to reclaim it when good times return.

Retain your authenticity. Putting down the mask of command at times may feel like a loss of control, but it adds to your credibility. If you're always playing a role, chances are that others will perceive you as a phony and wonder what you're concealing. Show that you're comfortable in your own skin and you'll gain trust that will last through difficult times. Share your beliefs, feelings, and convictions with your team, and ask about those of others. Character is more powerful than charisma. Show that an inner compass guides your actions.

The success of the CBS television series *Undercover Boss,* in which CEOs are disguised and then placed in entry level jobs in their company, is in part due to placing executives in situations that humble them. These CEOs are taken out of their comfort zones and put into jobs where they're bound to flounder. Yet their willingness to humble themselves in that manner boosts, rather than diminishes, their stature. The efforts by the show's producers to link the personal troubles of employees to the personal lives of the executives, removes the executive aura while showcasing their authenticity. Far more than charisma, authenticity wins over employees and viewers.

Beta leaders shouldn't get too high or too low. In a Beta organization victories and defeats are shared. Rather than establishing blame, conduct postmortems rather than inquisitions with an eye toward future improvements. Beware of hubris and overreach, both personally and as an organization. Rather than focusing on what individuals have achieved, concentrate on what has been achieved throughout the organization. Take collective pride in *everyone's* efforts.

In ancient Rome great heroes were celebrated with a triumph: a grand festival and parade. The conquering hero rode through the city in a chariot, with cheering crowds calling his name and tossing flowers in his path. Standing behind him in the chariot were two individuals. One held a laurel wreath over the hero's head, symbolizing his great achievements and honor. The other spent the ride whispering the same thing, over and over, into the hero's ear: "Remember, all fame is fleeting." That was Rome's way to remind its naturally Alpha leaders that they needed to manage their egos.

While the managed ego and productive narcissism of Beta leadership are the best approach for companies to succeed in the Information Age, that doesn't mean that command-and-control leadership should be entirely eliminated.

The one advantage an Alpha-style leader will always hold over her Beta counterpart is strategic speed. When decision-making power is held by one person or a small group, choices can be made very quickly, which can be vital in a crisis. Many existing Beta leaders found themselves temporarily transforming into Alphas in order to steer their companies through the Great Recession.

It's worth remembering: Betas are not weak. Far from it. There are times when a company screws up, or makes a misstep, or things go just plain wrong. It can happen to all kinds of businesses, from a traditional, white-shoe organization to a cutting-edge Internet company. Beta is not about ruling or deciding by committee; it does not absolve a single person from making decisions. No, Beta is about *knowing* when to take control, or set a new path, or embrace a new opportunity, which is why successful Beta leaders are constantly monitoring the organization and jumping in as circumstances dictate.

I once worked at a company under an all-powerful Alpha leader. The business was doing well, but we all recognized it could have been creating even more value for its stakeholders. I was tasked with finding a Beta leader who could enhance the organization, as opposed to coming in, pulverizing the institution with a hammer, and rebuilding it from scratch. In the end, I found an industry leader to fill the position. Before he started, I onboarded him with a specific mandate: There are some very good people in this organization, I told him. They may not work directly under you, but take time getting to know them. It's vital that you avoid coming in with all your guns blazing. I'm happy to say he didn't. Instead, he went around on a "Listening Tour," getting to know everyone in the organization. His approach was more community organizer than there's-a-new-sheriff-in-town. He was learning the business himself, he told people, and the executive suite was always open to anyone with a problem or a solution. Over the next few weeks and months, whenever his team would present him with data or other inputs and ask him how he wanted to proceed, invariably he would thank them for their work, then turn the tables around: "What do you recommend that we do as an organization with this data—and why?" By doing so, he raised the bar for everyone.

He didn't fire even a single person. Instead, he hired four new employees to enhance the senior team, creating new functions that didn't exist before. His changes were strategic, akin to rearranging lawn chairs on a deck. After all, the company was making money. Nothing in it was broken. It just wasn't working as efficiently as it could. Now, if the business were beginning to bleed, it might have benefited from a turnaround expert, a command-and-control guy. Could this guy have carried that out as well as anyone else? Absolutely. He may have been intrinsically a Beta manager, but he was fully capable of receiving data from employees, and rather than asking them how they would proceed, making hard decisions on the spot.

Which brings up another point: No Beta skill set would be complete without the capacity to listen. If listening sounds easy, it's not, as many people who have had conversations with CEOs will attest. Leaders are generally focused not on listening, but on figuring out what comes next. Yet, when it comes right down to it, listening is an essential function of any leader's skill set. In an era of data-driven decisions, most CEOs receive highly filtered information— "What did you hear him say?" is a common question people ask following a meeting with the boss—before giving out similar fact-based information. (From my perspective, future leaders need to be trained to analyze and mine a broad swath of widespread incoming data in order to match the strategy of the organization.)

Good listeners are conscious listeners. They clear their minds of biases and potential rebuttals. They make a conscious decision to process whatever it is they are hearing. They give the other party their genuine, undivided attention. They not only grasp what others are telling them, but they are also able to communicate it back. They provide feedback by paraphrasing, asking follow-up questions, clarifying certain points, or summarizing what they have just been told. They are also aware of the importance of nonverbal communication, whether it's a nod, a smile, a yawn, or a grimace. To my mind, conscious listening is a way to gather both information and perspective and to assert your response with honesty and respect.

As I mentioned above, sometimes Beta leaders must grab the reins and take control, especially in a time of crisis. Alternately, acknowledging the magnitude of the situation, a group of Beta leaders in an organization might decide to come together and choose one from their midst to become the Alpha to steer the company to safer waters. *First Among the Leadership Team* is what matters.

When Beta leaders need to deal with a crisis, however, they do so in a way that's different from typical Alpha decision-making. They may make command-and-control decisions, but they explain why. They take the time to communicate during the crisis, and ask for contributions from the entire organization, emphasizing that while everyone is in this together, they need to act rapidly. Thanks to information technology, it doesn't take a great deal of time or effort to communicate. In a crisis, the regular monthly visits and "town halls" at company facilities can be replaced by a broadcast e-mail or a single teleconference. Then, when the crisis is over, the command-and-control model can give way to the more collaborative, communicative, curatorial Beta model.

One model for taking charge in a crisis, before returning to being first among equals, is George Washington. After the American colonies won their independence from Great Britain, not everyone was convinced democracy was the best path to follow. Many army officers, long frustrated by the inefficiencies of the Continental Congress, urged their general, George Washington, to proclaim himself king. Washington certainly had the stature, bearing, and power to do so. But he was a Beta who had only donned an Alpha mantle to win the war. He gently rebuked his officers, subordinated himself to Congress, then left the army and returned to his farm as soon as possible. Years later, after the Articles of Confederation were replaced by the Constitution, and Washington had served two terms as president, he was urged to run again and become de facto president for life. Again, Washington gave up his temporary Alpha position and went back to Mount Vernon and private life. I can think of no better example of an individual with a managed ego and productive narcissism.

NINE

IT TAKES TWO TO BETA

It takes two to speak the truth—
one to speak, and another to hear.

—HENRY DAVID THOREAU

Alpha tendencies are hard to overcome, which isn't surprising. After all, Alpha has been the dominant paradigm in society for centuries, and most people who've reached the executive suite learned their lessons in Alpha organizations. Even those who've found the need to take a Beta approach, and who are working hard to transform their organizations, can reflexively fall back into Alpha patterns. More than once I've had a CEO, newly converted to the Beta approach, tell me, "I'm going turn this into a Beta organization if I have to do it myself."

The irony is hard to miss when you're not sitting in the corner office. I'm reminded of the army major who, during the Vietnam War, told the Associated Press's Peter Arnett that, "It became necessary to destroy the town to save it." Using an Alpha approach to create a Beta organization is as likely to succeed as that unnamed major's efforts were to pacify the town of Ben Tre. This is a case when the means have to be in sync with the end result.

First things first. Having a team of supportive direct reports and managers who buy into the Beta approach is vital. It's this executive team that provides the first level of collaboration that sparks the entire organization thinking and working together. But even more important than having a solid team of Betas onboard is having a junior partner who can be a co-agent of change.

Business relationships, particularly executive partnerships, are as singular as marriages. And while each has a complex, multilevel dynamic, successful Beta junior partners can be divided into four general types: Right Hands, Missing Pieces, Consigliere, and Heirs Apparent.

The Right Hand is the classic second-in-command who serves as the CEO's all-purpose subordinate. For some CEOs, the Right Hand serves as a chief of staff, freeing up the CEO of her administrative and political responsibilities to focus on strategy. For others, the Right Hand is the alter ego of the CEO, a person who can provide input and render some level of decisions in the CEO's place. Every Right Hand can also serve as acting CEO, assuming leadership on a short-term basis whenever necessary.

Whenever I counsel organizations, sure, the CEO may have brought me in, but invariably a so-called Palace Guard is in place. It could be the chief of staff, the management committee, or even an executive secretary. The buck rarely if ever stops with the CEO. For many years, Right Hand Dick Costolo worked alongside co-founder Evan Williams at Twitter. During his time as Twitter CEO, Williams scaled the company by dramatically increasing user numbers, and bringing celebrities and companies into the fold. Meanwhile, Costolo, an early Twitter investor and a former product manager at Google, carried out Williams's mission by spearheading Twitter's advertising initiatives. As I mentioned earlier, when Williams stepped down to focus again on product development, Dick

Costolo was poised to transform an influential communications platform into an equally influential advertising platform.

One of the greatest Right Hands in business history has to be Charlie Munger, the longtime partner of famed investor and Berkshire Hathaway CEO, Warren Buffett. Munger is little known outside the business community, and he prefers it that way, too. But if Buffett is the folksy, steely public face of Berkshire, Munger is his barbed sidekick, confidant, kindred spirit, and intellectual sparring partner. Munger may serve as Berkshire Hathaway's vice-chairman, but his unofficial company role is Buffett's co-strategist, even "co-thinker." The two men have been joined at the head and the wallet since 1982.

To this day, Buffett will still not make a single business decision without consulting his vice-chairman. Their collective brain trust creates the core of Berkshire Hathaway, a multinational that owns everything from GEICO Insurance to Fruit of the Loom textiles to See's Candies. Munger was once quoted as saying, "Warren knows an amazing amount, and he thinks very rapidly, and he talks very persuasively. I'm very similar in many ways. You get two people like that who really like and trust one another, and have been together for a long time, you're going to learn a lot from each other, and you're going to advance faster. So the learning machine is working faster."[1] From all reports, Munger plays the role of censor, contrarian, interrogator, and pessimist to Buffett's inveterate optimist. Not least, Munger is the only guy at Berkshire Hathaway who Buffett relies on to tell him the truth. Buffett has gone on record as saying that when CEOs surround themselves with yes-men, they invariably crash and burn. Over the years, Charlie Munger has helped to ensure this doesn't happen.

Among the many reasons the partnership works, Munger says, is that outside Berkshire Hathaway, he serves in countless activities where he is the dominant personality—the Alpha, if you will. He runs his own Los Angeles law firm. He sits on the boards of companies. Says Munger, "Most people do not 'fit into' that [secondary] mode—they can only operate in that mode. Yet I am particularly willing to play the secondary role. Warren's a more able man in doing what we're doing, so it's the appropriate response. There are some times you should be first, some times you should be second, and some times you should be third."[2] Buffett agrees that Munger has no issues serving in the number-two spot. The only disagreements the two men have, he notes, are intellectual; and even then they never spiral into contention. The Buffett-Munger relationship is a good reminder that the Right Hand man role works best in partnerships where one man seeks the spotlight, and the other does everything he can to duck it. At the company's annual meetings, Buffett fields questions from shareholders in his witty, rambling way. When he's done answering a question, he always asks Munger for his two cents. Munger's invariable reply: "I have nothing to add."

Then there's Disney's Michael Eisner and Frank Wells. Eisner recalls the time he spent working alongside Wells as the most successful, satisfying decade of his career. Like Munger, Frank Wells was himself a leader, a man who in most aspects of his life was unused to playing second fiddle. (A former Rhodes scholar, Wells was an accomplished lawyer and movie executive, as well as a mountain climber who'd made it his personal mission to climb the tallest peaks in every continent in the world.)

Originally Eisner and Wells were appointed co-CEOs of Disney, with Eisner tasked to head up the creative division, and Wells governing the business side. Eisner balked at this plan, which is when Wells spoke up. He was perfectly okay, he said, going forward in the company as Disney president and COO, with Eisner as Disney's sole chairman and CEO. (Over the next few years, Eisner repeatedly asked Wells why he stepped aside without putting up a fight. According to Eisner, "The answer [Frank] always gave me was almost too simple. He said any disagreement at that point would have kept us from getting off on the right foot.")[3]

As with Buffett and Munger, Eisner savored his role as Disney's public face, whereas Wells did not. (Wells practically exemplifies the term, *managed ego*.) Instead, Frank Wells was someone Disney employees went to for advice or counsel, or when something was going wrong in the company. He had formidable people skills. He handled any and all personnel issues. He finessed company politics. And, recalls Eisner, he was instrumental in helping shape Disney's attempts at synergy—creating a sequel of a successful film, which could then morph into a TV series, which could then become a toy in a Disney Store, which could then become a Disneyland ride or attraction. Wells stood alongside Eisner when the CEO decided to build new hotels at the company's theme parks, and move movie animation forward into digital. "No one could get between us," Eisner remembers. "How many companies have crumbled because of tension and weak relationships between people at the top of the company? At Disney, every meeting I was in, Frank heard about from me afterward. Every meeting he was in, he'd tell me about."[4] Frank Wells died in a helicopter crash in 1994, devastating everyone in the company, especially Eisner. During his memorial service, the former CEO recalls, Wells's son showed him a fortune from a fortune cookie he had found in his father's wallet. It read: "Humility is the final achievement."

Brian Grazer and Ron Howard operate one of the most successful producer-director teams in Hollywood. Their company, Imagine Films, is responsible for films ranging from *Splash* to *Apollo 13* to *A Beautiful Mind* to *Frost/Nixon* to *The Da Vinci Code*. Both passionate and competitive, the two men are otherwise opposites in just about every way. Grazer is the wild-haired, black-suited, restaurant-prowling Hollywood dealmaker. Howard prefers to stay on the East Coast with his family. Grazer is the guy manning the phones in the company's LA offices. Howard can often be found on location shooting a film. In business dealings with lawyers and business managers, Grazer plays the Bad Cop, while Howard is the first to admit he lacks his partner's combativeness and nerve. The two men never raise their voices at each other. They never parcel out blame. They split their earnings fifty-fifty. And early on in their relationship, they made a firm agreement: They didn't have to agree on the feasibility of every single project. They simply had to have the other's backing and support. That, says Howard, is the foundation of their partnership—well, that and the fact that professionally and personally, each one fills in what the other lacks.

Dwight Eisenhower, whose leadership of Allied forces in Europe during World War II was more akin to a CEO than a field general, was savvy enough to enlist the services of the ultimate Right Hand: General Walter Bedell Smith. Smith was able to serve as Eisenhower's "hatchet man" and deliver bad news to powerful personalities such as Generals Patton and Montgomery, as well as serving as Ike's personal representative on sensitive diplomatic missions. Smith eventually went on to serve as head of the CIA for both Presidents Truman and Eisenhower.

The Missing Piece supplies skills and expertise the CEO lacks. Beta CEOs tend to be more willing to admit and acknowledge their lack of expertise and hire someone to help fill the gap. In Alpha organizations, odds are that CEOs wouldn't want to draw attention to their flaws and would perceive someone who possesses those skills as a potential threat. A Missing Piece automatically provides an added perspective for a CEO, paving the way for more collaborative decision-making.

The history of the luxury handbag brand, Coach, underscores

the importance of the Missing Piece in a company's evolution. Founded in 1941 under the name Manhattan Leather Bags, Coach's first handbags were inspired by high-quality baseball gloves. (You read that right, and no, the ball was not included.) It wasn't until two decades later that Coach began to resemble the organization, and the product, that it does today. Three Missing Pieces played a part. In the early 1960s, Coach hired Bonnie Cashin, a pioneer in importing industrial hardware—including such rough-hewn materials as leather straps—onto sportswear. Under Cashin's guidance, Coach began producing bags with brass hardware, and began advertising in upscale urban periodicals like *The New Yorker*.

But it wasn't until the company brought in Missing Piece Lew Frankfort, today the company CEO, that Coach reached its potential. When Coach hired Frankfort, there was no midpriced handbag available on the market; consumers had to choose between third-rate knockoffs and expensive designer totes. Today, Frankfort is credited as the man who steered Coach to its new platform as an aspirational—but affordable—global luxury brand. Under his stewardship, the company began publishing a catalog, and also opened a flagship in Midtown Manhattan. In time the company went on to manufacture watches, raincoats, and trench coats, while also expanding successfully into Japan. But there was one last Missing Piece that needed to be filled.

A sportswear designer and Tommy Hilfiger veteran, Reed Krakoff joined Coach in 1996 and in 1999 was named president, executive creative director. Under his leadership, Coach morphed from a reliable collection of briefcases to a continuously evolving line of stylish new colors and designs. In 2001, the company rolled out its Signature line, followed, five years later, by its Legacy collection, which incorporated suede and canvas, a palette of new colors and magnets rather than toggles to seal the bags. When Krakoff joined Coach, it was a half-billion-dollar company. Under his direction, the company blossomed into a global conglomerate currently valued at $4 billion. Today, Krakoff has his own eponymous, and wildly successful, Coach fashion line.

Vice-presidential candidates chosen by American political parties are classic examples of Missing Pieces. Typically, a president selects a candidate to provide certain elements that the president himself lacks—whether it's an appeal to small-town voters, a desirable demographic base, youthfulness, or gravitas. A young presidential candidate typically selects an experienced elder statesman or stateswoman as his running mate. An Easterner may pair up with a candidate from a different part of the country, or a moderate may select a running mate favored by the more ideological members of his party.

The Consigliere is the unbiased advisor, offering input and insights with no personal agenda. It's this lack of bias that makes the Consigliere so effective. Usually he's a seasoned executive who's not a likely candidate to replace the CEO, or she's an outside consultant with no possibility of taking the helm. The Consigliere's focus is on being an advocate for the Beta approach, as either a chief talent officer or a special advisor to the CEO.

The term *consigliere* came into the American lexicon thanks to Francis Ford Coppola's Godfather trilogy. In the first two films, the leader of the Corleone crime family, played by Marlon Brando, has as his unbiased advisor, Tom Hagen, an attorney. As an Irish, nonfamily member, Hagen isn't a possible successor to the Don. As a result, his advice is uncontaminated by self-interest. Michael Corleone, played by Al Pacino, temporarily replaces Hagen as Consigliere with his now retired father, who also isn't influenced by self-interest.

Defined as someone who is ambitious, but whose ambition is part of a managed ego, and doesn't exhibit itself sheerly for ambition's sake, Consiglieri exist in just about every organization. It could be the head of human resources who over time becomes a business partner. It could be the company COO, the CFO, a division president or the head of marketing, an individual who genuinely understands the CEO and the company, but who has no interest in spreading his wings across broader areas of the organization. A Consigliere holds up an essential mirror to the CEO. They may not be directly *in* the game, but they understand the rules and the players and what's at stake, and their big-shouldered perspective allows them to advise and counsel those who are. Among other things, a Consiglere's role is to help others turn up the volume of their very best. To revisit our orchestra analogy, a Consigliere is a formidable player—a virtuoso, even—who knows that by helping others in the organization, he can achieve his own goals.

If you think it's easy being a Consigliere to a powerful CEO, think again. A Consigliere practically defines "managed ego." Advising the most powerful man or woman in a company requires an enormous amount of self-reflection and self-awareness. Does the Consigliere have the very best intentions for the business? Is he in it for self-glorification? How pure are his motivations? As I wrote earlier, CEOs are the most isolated people on earth. They are under constant pressure from shareholders, corporate boards, the media, and government regulators, not to mention their own families who wonder why they are never around. At work, they have no real peers, no true colleagues. Just about everyone in their immediate orbit has a bias, or an agenda. Time Warner CEO Richard Parsons was once quoted as saying, "For years, [Time Warner CEO] Gerry Levin was one of the guys here I was closest to, but there were certain issues I was reluctant to bring up to him because he was the CEO. . . . So I have to assume the same thing is happening with the people who work for me."[5]

Which is one reason why the extremely low-profile Bill Campbell is such an influential figure in Silicon Valley. As a background advisor to such business figures as John Doerr, Steve Jobs, and Google's ex-CEO Eric Schmidt, Campbell has long been considered a stealth weapon for some of the best-known companies in the world. Schmidt has said he literally cannot overstate Campbell's contributions to Google. Other CEOs have praised Campbell's humanity, his honesty, and his ambition to create strong, long-lasting companies. As the former chairman and CEO of Intuit, whose revenue Campbell more than doubled, and a current member of Apple's board of directors, Campbell helped Google set up a product management group, advised Schmidt on how best to conduct staff meetings, counseled him on hiring, and helped bring together Google's board of directors. When Google bought YouTube in 2006, Campbell stepped up to advise CEO Chad Hurley on how best to maintain the company's corporate culture. Two decades earlier, when Apple was first making its presence known in personal computing, Campbell pushed the company to broadcast its Ridley Scott–directed "1984" ad during the Super Bowl, a watershed moment that introduced the Macintosh personal computer to the world. Campbell ultimately helped transform Apple's software unit, Claris, into a $100 million division, while at the same time mentoring the future co-founders of Palm and Handspring, and the future founder of Adobe Systems.

The Heir Apparent is the designated successor, a person being groomed by the CEO and the board to eventually take the place of the current CEO. While the Heir Apparent may at times serve as a Right Hand, or initially serve as a Missing Piece, it's likely he or she will be as much student as advisor. The Heir Apparent's role is to absorb the lessons already learned by the CEO, and to acquire the skills and knowledge needed to take the organization to the next level. That could mean taking on a variety of assignments, or it could mean sitting at the elbow of the CEO, and through questioning, serve as a sounding board for decisions.

At different developmental stages of a company, leaders have to decide about what a company needs next. Yet instead of carrying out a needs assessment, most conduct an external search, which, from my perspective, often risks pushing a company's evolution back a year or more. Why? Because it takes that long for an outsider to become acculturated. A good analogy would be when friends' marriages unravel. Countless men and women make the mistake of quickly remarrying, often to the same kind of person they just left. Betas are great for positioning for further growth, while Alphas are great in times of crisis. Somewhere in between lies true horizontal leadership—such as that shown by the new CEO Apple appointed after Steve Jobs's death, former company COO and Heir Apparent Tim Cook. Though Cook originally came to Apple as an expert on manufacturing, serving as a Missing Piece for the design and marketing genius Steve Jobs, he eventually became Jobs's Right-Hand man. When Jobs was forced to take leaves of absence for health reasons throughout the 1990s and 2000s, Cook became acting CEO, filling in without the company missing a beat. With each successful stint as acting CEO, Cook became the obvious Heir Apparent. When Jobs resigned to become Apple's chairman, Cook took over amid little more than reflexive concern. And when Jobs died, Cook's hand on the tiller, then and now, has kept the company on its successful course.

I'm forever surprised by how few Beta CEOs take the time to select a co-change agent. So much effort and attention is focused on team building and the creation of collaborative processes that few CEOs set aside the time needed to find an internal partner. Perhaps they perceive it as being too self-serving, and overly Alpha, at a time when they're looking to instill a Beta ethos in the organization. But in fact, a co-change agent can help the Beta process by serving as a confidential sounding board for the CEO, and an intermediary for other executives and managers who may feel uncomfortable discussing certain issues with the CEO. A co-change agent in a certain kind of company can be a sage hiring decision. If a few years ago, Barnes & Noble told me they were looking for someone to help enhance the company, I would not have sent them a book business veteran. Instead, I would have found them someone who understood where the future of electronic books, and digital content, was heading. If YouTube needs a high-level executive, why hire an outsider who knows the ins and outs of video? That ship, after all, has sailed. Instead, why not bring in an expert in television programming or advertising sales? At different points in its life, a company's pivot points, and needs, change. It may sound simple, but it seldom is. I like to say that business is extremely commonsensical, except for all the people involved.

The first step in finding a partner is deciding what type you need. If you're feeling stretched too thin by your simultaneous efforts to run and transform your organization, find a Right-Hand man. If an honest self-assessment or unbiased advice highlights your need to fill a gap in your expertise or knowledge, be on the lookout for a Missing Piece. If your current team is well qualified, but you're eager for some coaching and guidance to make the Beta transition, find a Consigliere. And if you feel the process is well on its way, and you're beginning to experience wanderlust, look for an Heir Apparent.

Next, decide whether you should look inside or outside your organization. Right Hands and Consiglieri often come from outside the organization as they benefit from political independence and a fresh perspective. Missing Pieces and Heirs Apparent can come from inside or outside, depending on the makeup of the current executive team and the plans of the CEO and board.

But whatever kind of partner you bring onboard, and wherever you find him or her, be prepared to compensate and motivate them appropriately. This isn't a short-term choice. Even if you're bringing in a consultant to serve as a Consigliere, you need that person to make a long-term commitment to you and the organization, to see you both through the entire transformative process. Today, besides compensation, it's equally important to keep your partner engaged and challenged.

You don't need to transform your organization alone. And if you want to create a Beta organization you shouldn't do it by yourself, either. A co-change agent can make the process easier for you and better for your company.

TEN

CHASING MENTORS AND MOTIVATED SKILLS

*If I have seen further than others, it is by standing
upon the shoulders of giants.*

—Isaac Newton

For most of the twentieth century, Americans were strikingly consistent in the way they approached their careers. All that changed two decades ago. Since then, the rules and the tenor of the contemporary workplace have undergone a series of profound transformations. In the age of Beta, the only thing we can say for sure about career management is that no single, cookie-cutter model exists. Today's workers have to individually craft and manage their own professional paths.

Which brings me back to the two businesses and models that we visited back in chapter 1. The first one we called Alpha. The second we dubbed Beta. The question is, if you happen to be a talented Information Age worker, which company would you rather work for?

I recently counseled a thirty-one-year-old woman who faced this same choice. A skilled sales and marketing executive, Sarah graduated from a West Coast university and got her MBA from an East Coast business school. She was smart, accomplished, and ambitious, and she and her husband, a consultant, had just had their second child.

Sarah's first interview was at an Alpha organization. Before she went in, the only thing on Sarah's mind was finding a good fit for her proven strengths in sales and social media. She sought an environment where her colleagues were receptive to her ideas, where the feedback was targeted and continuous, where her department and others could collaborate on new initiatives, and where she had a strong personal stake (financial *and* psychological) in the company's future growth and success.

But her experience at the Alpha organization put her off. The place felt old-fashioned, buttoned-down in a way that felt out of step with who she was. The employees seemed happy enough, yet no one appeared to share a common goal or mission. Asking around, she discovered that none of the employees had an equity stake in the company. There was little if any flextime. What's more, if she ended up taking the position, her direct superiors would work out of an office twelve floors above her own. The digital division, with which she'd be working closely, was four floors below. There was a distinct feeling of rivalry in the air. Sarah was reminded of a lecture that entrepreneur and PayPal founder Peter Thiel had delivered at Stanford University. Thiel suggested that competition—and the competitive enviroment it fostered—went so far as to *inhibit* creativity. That company employees were so busy competing with one another, as well as with their business rivals, that they forgot about what innovation really means, namely, risk-taking and creating new paths in untraditional markets.

The Alpha environment just didn't fit with who Sarah was, what she knew, or where she wanted to go.

Inside the Beta organization, it was a different story. On first glance the place may have looked disordered, but it wasn't, not at all. It was dressed-down, kinetic, informal. Everyone was on a first name basis with everyone else. Managers sat around chatting with staffers. Across the hall, two employees were playing a fierce game of Foosball. Mistaking her for a colleague, one man even handed her an application for an employee mini-marathon, with the proceeds going to a local cancer research hospital.

During the first of three interviews, Sarah was struck by the company's focus on fostering innovation, to the point of insisting that all employees devote at least two days a month to their own professional initiatives. The interviewer couldn't have cared less what university Sarah had attended. She focused instead on Sarah's personality—her enthusiasm, her curiosity, her ability and willingness to collaborate, and whether she and the culture were a potentially good match. She asked Sarah to put her expectations on the table. "What is it you *want?*" the interviewer said, adding, with a smile, "and then we'll tell you what *we* want—because in the end, we can help each other." Which freed Sarah up to define exactly what she was looking for, and for the Human Resources executive to do the same.

In addition to the medical, dental, vision, and disability—and the thirty-five-hour workweek, which the company claimed actually *increased* productivity—Sarah was impressed by the company "extras." There was a recreation and fitness center. A day care. A medical center that provided free health care free to all employees and their families. (At a cost of $4.5 million, the medical center had already paid for itself, since employees didn't waste time driving to doctors' appointments, or hanging around in waiting rooms.) There was a hairdresser, a dry cleaner, and a post office. Lobby posters advertised workplace stress-reduction programs, including massage, yoga, meditation, hiking, aerobics, and weight management. New parents were granted a five-hundred-dollar take-out meal fund from the company's three cafeterias. A stand-alone "Work-Life" department gave staffers advice and counsel about elder care; debt management; adoption; raising adolescents; and how to become a healthier, happier person. The company also offered an education leave initiative, which reimbursed employees up to $150,000 if they chose to pursue an advanced degree.

Sarah left the interview convinced that she and the company were after the same things. Both believed that treating people well was more important than making a few extra bucks. Both believed that employees wanted to be seen, heard, and now and again, thanked. Both believed that employees needed to be given the opportunity to make a difference—to give input into key decisions, to communicate their findings and learnings with senior people. Both believed that a manager's biggest responsibility was to help his employees succeed. Finally, both believed that most employees wanted to work for a CEO who was a visionary and a leader, rather than a PR microphone for Wall Street or for the board.

In the lobby was a small plaque spelling out the differences between a "boss" and a "leader." A boss drives employees; relies on authority; inspires fear; says "I"; places blame for breakdowns; uses people; takes credit; commands; and says "go." In contrast, a leader coaches his employees; generates enthusiasm; says "we"; fixes breakdowns; shows how it is done; develops people; gives credit; asks; and says "Let's go."

In the end, both companies ended up offering Sarah a job. She'd already made up her mind.

As I hope this book has shown, workplaces and workforces are evolving fast, which has made my work as a corporate anthropologist busy, challenging, and exhilarating. Today we find ourselves living in an environment so radically dissimilar from past times it is almost comical. As Sarah's experience shows, today's workers bring far different histories and expectations to the table and to the workplace than previous generations did. Information Age employees are global in their perspectives, and have a strong stake in the state of the earth. Today, "Cause-Related Marketing" is a growing phenomenon, whether it's Procter & Gamble joining forces with UNICEF to provide vaccines to eradicate neonatal tetanus in forty-seven countries, or California-based shoemaker, Toms, pledging to donate a pair of shoes to a child in need every time a consumer makes a purchase. But cause-related marketing is more than a PR stunt. Sarah told me that she and her Information Age peers care deeply about what a business stands for as an organization, and that it treat its people not as assets, or "social capital," but as investments.

Today's winning organizations must ensure that their people flourish in their functions. Corporations who are helplessly stuck in old cultures, who pay attention to customers while turning their backs on their own employees, forget that their customers *are* their employees.

Will we ever return to the old Alpha standard? The thing is, we can't. Successive generations will follow the model of their own parents, and their parents' workplaces. The most successful organizations of the future are those that can find, attract, and retain the very best talent. And that same talent is now responsible for sculpting its own professional futures.

A few years ago, I had to learn this lesson myself.

The company I was running had just been sold, and I was given the opportunity to take a management position that would pay me a good salary and give me an equity position in a larger, very successful, established human resources consulting company. I was also offered a chance to become involved in a venture capital firm, alongside some extremely successful individuals. All my personal advisors encouraged me to think conservatively and build up my nest egg and equity in the large consulting company. But looking around, I saw how companies once perceived as "secure" were teetering on the edge, and how choices once dubbed as fail-safe were resulting in disaster. I thought about the people I could work with in venture capital, and how being in business with them would give me a chance to learn from brilliant people, and to continue developing the skills and abilities that gave me satisfaction. So instead of chasing the money, I chased mentors, and pursued my own motivated skills.

It was the best decision I've ever made. Since then, I've been counseling every single one of my clients, whether they are young people just starting out in business or experienced CEOs, to do precisely the same. Chase happiness and fulfillment. Look for joy and challenges. Take calculated risks that enhance your knowledge and your skills. Do what you are good at. The money will follow.

We are living and working in unstable times. Taking a strictly hierarchical, traditional approach to your career development makes no more sense than taking an Alpha approach to business management.

Today, you need to collaborate with a team of mentors and advisors and curate your own path. That means becoming aware of your strengths and weaknesses, your likes and dislikes, and realizing that like everybody, you need to grow and learn. Look for opportunities to be a high contributor, not just a high earner. Look for a community where you feel comfortable and valued. Take risks, in both moving on and staying put. Play to your strengths. If you feel you're in the wrong place, consider moving, even if the environment isn't conducive to changing jobs. If you feel you're in the right place, then do everything in your power to stay there. Keep score based on your professional development, not on your income or your status. When you pursue development, money will follow. Pursue money, and disappointment will follow. Don't lose your own identity by defining yourself by your employer.

If you're toward the end of your career, embrace rather than resist change. Let new situations invigorate you. Stop looking for what doesn't exist. Rewire your expectations. I've encouraged former construction managers to take jobs as managers at Lowe's while investigating home inspection franchises. And I've coached COOs, who were convinced they should take a new job only if it was a CEO position, to put aside titles and instead look to pursue their motivated skills. A COO whose advancement is stymied should be open to taking a position other than CEO or even COO, if it gives him or her a chance to do what provides self-actualization, or the opportunity to learn a suite of new skills.

Last year, a young executive came to me for advice on his next career step. He was the designated successor to the CEO of a well-known Fortune 1000 American brand, but felt stifled. He had always wanted to be the CEO of a global company, yet he also felt vulnerable. He had no acquisition or board experience. For him, it made sense to shift to a position with another smaller organization where he could grow a company and interact with a board. The thing is, he loved the company, was a great fit with its culture, got along well with the CEO and, as the parent of a young child, had no desire to move to a company where'd he have to become a road warrior.

Instead of encouraging him to make the jump, I urged him to take control of his own career development. *Why not approach the CEO with your dilemma?* I asked him. He did. Eager to retain him, the CEO promptly put him on the board, where he gradually acquired acquisition experience. By taking charge of his own career trajectory, acknowledging both his strengths and his weaknesses, and asking for an opportunity to contribute and learn at the same time, he achieved everything he wanted.

A few weeks after counseling the future CEO, I found myself coaching a recent college graduate who was working his first job. He'd gone to school for design and had landed a spot with a major media company. His work involved manipulating content so it looked attractive on the company's Web site. It was a job in his field, with a solid company, that paid him a good entry salary, at a time when many of his peers were unemployed or working as waitstaff in restaurants. Yet after only a few hours of conversation, both of us realized he needed to look elsewhere. He simply wasn't in a culture that would encourage his creativity since the company lacked a design orientation. Discussing his motivated skills and lack of mentors, it was obvious he'd have to leave eventually if he wanted to develop his career. I explained to him that he was better off leaving sooner rather than later. The longer he stayed, the harder it would become for him to change, and the longer he stayed, the more difficult it would be for other companies to view him as anything other than a creature of his employer.

Whether someone is just starting out, is one step from the corner office, or has one foot out the door to retire, it's vital they take charge of their own careers and personal development. There's no longer a single career model with the goal of the highest rung on the ladder. That kind of Alpha style approach no longer works. Besides, it offers little or no chance for self-actualization and satisfaction. An authentic Beta career is one in which you collaborate with your advisors, curate your own future, and place personal development over financial reward. Follow your bliss and the money will come.

EPILOGUE

The future belongs to the Betas, not the Alphas. It belongs to organizations and leaders who communicate, collaborate, and curate. These are exciting times—if you're willing to take the plunge. Here's how:

Organizations and leaders today should have as open a dialogue as possible, not just internally with employees, but also externally. Success demands that you be willing and able to collaborate with employees, directors, customers, and competitors. It demands that you encourage your teammates to play to their own strengths, and to pursue their own areas of interest and expertise, rather than forcing them to follow a predetermined development path. Understand that every individual in your organization is a contributor and has potential; and the closer everyone comes to self-actualization, the closer the organization comes to achieving its potential.

While you're at it, why not apply the same principles to your organization's development as you do to your own and that of your employees? Create a company that is a community rather than an army. Build shifting, project- or process-based teams rather than functional silos. Instead of chasing quarterly numbers and aiming to boost short-term revenue (and compensation), follow strategies that benefit the entire community through growth and long-term profitability.

Shift the goal to reaching the top of Maslow's Hierarcy of Needs pyramid rather than the Hierarchy of Titles pyramid. Get rid of elitism. Rather than focusing solely on those with the best numbers, reward your facilitators. Value your "craftspeople" as much as you do your managers. Practice ego management. Reward collaborative behavior and teamwork. Transform yourself into a productive narcissist, someone who tempers self-esteem and confidence with empathy and compassion. Finally, not least, practice mindfulness. Mindfulness, of self and of others, by executives and employees, may well be the single most important ingredient for a successful twenty-first-century company.

Everywhere I look, the world is going Beta. My advice? Join the movement before it's too late, and you'll find your organization succeeding beyond your wildest dreams.

ACKNOWLEDGMENTS

The difficult we do immediately. The impossible takes a little longer.

—U.S. Armed Forces (Jack Silverstein, distinguished WWII veteran)

To my parents, Fay and Jack Silverstein, who always gave me confidence, belief in myself and the world of possibilities. To my sister, Ilene Minskoff, for your love and support. To my nephews Evan, David, Bradley, and Mikey—I am always there to share your dreams. To my goddaughter, Rachel Botsman, who encouraged me to follow her example and write.

To my agent Henry Dunow for his excellent advice and counsel. To my editor, George Witte, who is dedicated and skilled. To Peter Smith and Mark Levine for their talents, perseverance, and patience to take my interviews and thoughts and organize them and me. I am so appreciative for you being my mentors through the project.

To Jeffrey Walker, Jonathan Miller, Gerry Lopez, Daniel Hamburger, and Steve Kerr for agreeing to be interviewed and sharing your ideas around leadership. You are all on my personal Board of Advisors, and I cannot thank you enough for inspiring me. To Fred Wilson who was interviewed for this book and is the Chairman of my personal Board and has always been there for me.

I could not have done this without the support of my family and friends. To Tina Sharkey and Liz Heller, the members of the "Girlfriend Summit"; to Caryn Fox my dear cousin, to Martina Sternfeld, Melissa Harris, Matti Leshem, Jeffrey Baymor, Brian and Elyse Napack—I would like to thank you for believing in me.

To all my colleagues who have shared their professional journey with me. To the Flatiron Partners (Fred Wilson, Jerry Colonna, Bob Greene), my colleagues at J.P. Morgan Partners and CCMP Capital, thank you for the lessons learned. You are all in my heart.

To my team who stands behind me at Corporate Anthropology Advisors and my lawyer, Barry Dastin of Kaye Scholer, thank you for helping me define the next chapter.

And finally, to all my clients—I get up each morning excited by the opportunities you provide and by the privilege to contribute to your growth and your futures.

ENDNOTES

One: Corporate Anthropology

1. Clare Longrigg, "Is There Any Such Thing as an Alpha Female?" *The Guardian,* September 21, 2003.
2. Ibid.
3. Doug Gross, "10 Years Later, Apple's 'Crazy' Retail Gamble Is a Hit," *CNN Tech,* May 18, 2011.
4. Yukari Iwatani Kane and Ian Serr, "Secrets from Apple's Genius Bar: Full Loyalty, No Negativity," *The Wall Street Journal,* June 15, 2011.
5. David Whitford, "Sandler O'Neill's Journey from Ground Zero," *Fortune,* September 5, 2011.
6. Charles Fishman, "Sabbaticals Are Serious Business," *Fast Company,* October 31, 1996.
7. Ibid., p. 151.
8. Sara Kehaulani Goo, "Building a 'Googley' Workforces," *The Washington Post,* October 21, 2006.
9. Ibid.
10. Ibid.
11. *http://www.aacsb.edu/publications/archives/novdec04/p16-21.pdf*
12. Ibid.
13. *http://www.thehiredguns.com/blogs/2012/03/15/why-your-employees-want -partnership/*

14. Adam Bryant, "What's Your Story? Tell It, and You May Win a Prize," *The New York Times*, April 21, 2012.
15. Ibid.
16. Ibid.
17. Matthew Boyle, "The Wegmans Way," *Fortune*, January 24, 2005.
18. Claire Cane Miller, "Why Twitter's CEO Demoted Himself," *The New York Times*, October 30, 2010.
19. Jennifer Reingold, "The Fall and Rise of David Pottruck," *Fast Company*, September 1, 2005.

Three: Boomers and Bonobos

1. Paco Underhill, *What Women Want: The Science of Female Shopping*, 2011, Simon & Schuster, New York, p. 13.
2. Ibid.
3. Liza Mundy, *The Richer Sex: How the New Majority of Female Breadwinners Is Transforming Sex, Love, and Family* (New York: Simon & Schuster, March, 2012), p. 7.

Five: Communication, Collaboration, and Curation

1. Brad Stone and Ashlee Vance, "Apple's Obsession with Secrecy Grows Stronger," *The New York Times*, June 22, 2009.
2. Ray Kurzweil, "The Law of Accelerating Returns," March 7, 2001, *http://www.kurzweilai.net/the-law-of-accelerating-returns*
3. E. J. Schultz, "Weight Watchers Picks a New Target: Men," *Crain's*, April 22, 2011.
4. Paul Hodgson, "Women on Boards: The Good News, There Are More. The Bad News, Not That Many," *Forbes*, March 8, 2012.
5. Ibid.
6. Ibid.
7. Bob Deutsch, Ph.D., "Harnessing the Power of Both Sexes on Corporate Boards," *Forbes*, November 17, 2011.
8. Ibid.
9. Ibid.
10. Helen McCormick, "Sustainability: Sprucing Up Corporate Social Responsibility with Timberland," *Personnel Today*, November 5, 2007.
11. Jennifer Reingold, "Walking the Walk," *Fast Company*, November 1, 2005, *http://www.fastcompany.com/magazine/100/timberland.html*

Six: The Top of a Different Pyramid

1. Abraham Maslow, *Motivation and Personality* (New York: Harper and Row Publishers, 1954), chapter 4.
2. Tony Hsieh, *Delivering Happiness: A Path to Profits, Passion, and Purpose* (New York: Business Plus, 2010), p. 136.
3. Ibid., p. 138.
4. Max Chafkin, "The Zappos Way of Managing," *Inc*, May 1, 2009.
5. *http://www.slapcompany.com/slap-training-programs/achieving-emotional -commitment-in-managers*
6. *http://www.fedex.com/ma/about/overview/philosophy.html*

Seven: Eliminating Elitism

1. Jennifer Reingold and Jia Lynn Yang, "The Hidden Workplace," *Fortune*, July 18, 2007.

Eight: Managing Ego

1. Carlson, Nicholas, "Larry Page Just Tied ALL Employees' Bonuses to the Success of Google's Social Strategy," *Business Insider*, April 7, 2011. *http:// www.businessinsider.com/larry-page-just-tied-employee-bonuses-to-the-success -of-the-googles-social-strategy-2011-4*

Nine: It Takes Two to Beta

1. Michael Eisner, *Working Together: Why Great Partnerships Succeed* (New York: Harper Business, 2010), p. 40.
2. Ibid., p. 46.
3. Ibid., p. 29.
4. Ibid., p. 25.
5. David Nadler, "Confessions of a Trusted Counselor," *Harvard Business Review*, September 2005.

INDEX

advisory boards, 106

Afghanistan, 134

Agricultural Age, 12, 57
  gender roles and, 53–55
  leadership, 55

airbrushing, 104

algorithmic work, 82

Alpha females
  1980s and 1990s, 12–14
  primate studies and, 62

Alpha leaders
  on board of directors, 116
  frustration and unhappiness in, 111–12
  Williams stepping down, 37–38

Alpha males
  Augustus as, 54
  concept, 11
  Elizabeth I as, 55–56
  primate studies and, 62, 74–75

Alpha model
  baby boomers haunted by, 40
  closed-door culture of, 96
  in different contexts, 99
  endurance of, 14–15
  entitlement sense, 84
  entrepreneurship and, 21–22
  external communication in, 96
  pyramid structure of, 79–82
  satisfaction failure, 130–31
  scientific studies and, 59–63, 74–75
  secrecy norm of, 90–91, 96
  social interactions impacted by, 64
  success judged by, 131–32

Alpha organizations
  army general analogy, 33–35
  Beta model being adopted by, 49
  Beta organizations compared to, 33–35
  career regimentation, 111
  elitism in, 140–44

Alpha organizations (*continued*)
    facilitator role in, 151
    floor plans, 2–3, 45, 148
    hypothetical, 1–5
    Sarah's interview with Beta and,
        202–4
    September 11 response of, 22
    transforming, 140, 149
Amazon.com, 20–21, 107
ambition
    CEO client's, 111–12
    horizontal, 36
AMC Entertainment Holdings, Inc.,
    96, 102
American Girl Doll, 145
American Idol, 31
Amerman, John, 145
androgen insensitivity, 76
angular employees, 28
AOL, 48, 148
Apple, Inc., 19
    alliances and collaborations of, 107
    Consigliere, 197
    Missing Piece, 198
    PARC visit to Apple Computers,
        82
    secrecy of, 90–91
apprenticeships, women denied, 46
archetype, Alpha male, 56
army general analogy, 33–35
Arnett, Peter, 188
Augustus, 54
authenticity, in leaders, 96–97
authoritarianism, 88

Baby Boom, 70
baby boomers, 40, 68
BabyCenter, 162
Barad, Jill, 144–46

Barbie doll, 144–46
Barkley, Charles, 131
Barnes & Noble, 199
Baumeister, Roy, 168
Beiber, Justin, 170
Ben Tre, 188
Berkshire Hathaway, 190–91
Beta career, curation, 119–20, 158
Beta culture, 1
Beta leaders
    capacity for understanding in,
        178–79
    change to becoming, 26–27
    characteristic defining, 18
    co-change agents for, 198–200
    during crisis, 186–87
    as curators, 17, 113–15
    ego management practiced by,
        27, 165
    grandmother as, 43–44
    managers, 154
    mission established by, 174
    motivated skills of, 16–17
    September 11 response of, 23–25
    Sullivan as example of, 42, 44, 51
Beta model
    Alpha organizations adopting, 49
    customer input in, 103–6
    decision-making by CEO, 97–98
    definition of, 89
    human nature and, 35
    as not democracy, 97
    orchestra analogy, 33–35, 114, 165
    in personal lives, 39–40
    success variations in, 119–20
Beta organizations
    Alpha compared to, 33–35
    Alpha organizations shifting to
        become, 49

C-level positions created in, 158
clients as start-up, 48–49
company-wide understanding in,
    177–78
employee interests aligned in, 50
examples of, 26–33
hypothetical example, 5–9
as learning organizations, 157, 160
organization chart, 7–8, 165–66
requirement for building, 26
Sarah's interview with Alpha and,
    202–4
September 11 response of, 22
snacks eliminated by, 22
Bezos, Jeff, 20–21
biology, gender and, 77
Blackwell, Elizabeth, 57
Blaffer Hrdy, Sarah, 74
boards of directors
    CEO leaving meetings, 174
    CEO support from, 118–19
    curatorial approach needed by, 115
    gender quotas for, 117
    member recruitment, 119
    women on, 116–18
Bock, Laszlo, 29
Bonelia, 75
Bonfire of the Vanities, The (Wolfe), 69
bonobos, 74–75
Bootlegging Hour, 129
bottlenecks, in social network
    analysis, 152
Boyle, Susan, 87
Brady, Tom, 14–15
brains, gender studies on, 77
Brando, Marlon, 195
brokers, in social network analysis,
    152
Brown, Tim, 138

Buffett, Warren, 190–91
*Bury My Heart at Conference Room B:
    The Unbeatable Impact of Truly
    Committed Managers*, 136
Butterball Turkey Talk Line, 98–99

Campbell, Bill, 196–97
Campbell, Jim (hypothetical CEO),
    6, 7, 8
campus presidents, 155
career path, 43
    curation of Beta, 119–20, 158
    gender statistics, 59
    managing own, 201, 206–8
    negative side of following
        established, 155
    regimented and predestined, 111
    self-awareness and, 37–38
Carlin, George, 11
Cashin, Bonnie, 194
Catmull, Edwin, 29
causes
    cause-related marketing, 205
    unity through social, 178–79
CCMP Capital, 43
CDs, 169–70
CEO. *See* Chief Executive Officer
CFO. *See* Chief Financial Officer
Chappell, Tom, 161
Charles Schwab, 38–39
Chief Executive Officer (CEO)
    Alpha position let go of by, 37–38
    ambitious client, 111–12
    average job tenure for, 107
    board meetings left by, 174
    board support for, 118–19
    CEO-in-Waiting, 46–47
    Charles Schwab, 38–39
    client seeking replacement, 93–95

Chief Executive Officer (*continued*)
  communication style changes for, 84
  compensation and equity share, 157
  compensation ratio of employees to, 148
  competition between two direct reports set up by, 109–10
  Consigliere, 195–97, 199–200
  decision-making by, 97–98
  direct reports, 189
  employees empowered by, 174–75
  in entry level jobs, 182
  facilitator role of, 152–53
  go-to guy for, 132–33
  Heir Apparent, 197–98, 199
  hypothetical company #1, 3, 4–5
  hypothetical company #2, 6, 7, 8
  isolation of, 107–9
  Jack Welch-style, 99
  Missing Piece, 193–95, 199
  notebook kept by, 114
  offices of typical Alpha, 2–3
  praise from, 156
  preparation for position of, 146
  Right Hand, 189–93
  Rosen as, 3, 4–5
  social media dismissed by, 172–73
  Starbucks, 101–2
Chief Financial Officer (CFO), "Sam," 36–37
Chief Operations Officer (COO), 165, 196
  Disney's, 191
  motivated skills as priority for, 207
  Twitter's former, 37–38
Child, Lee, 21
Choe, David, 33
chromosomal assessment, 76–77

City National Bank, 30–31
Claris, 197
C-level positions, 4, 158
clients
  ambitious CEO, 111–12
  CEO replacement search, 93–95
  graduate on first job, 207–8
  Sarah's interviews with Alpha and Beta companies, 202–4
closed-door culture, 95
CNN, 152
Coach, 193–95
co-change agents, 198–200
Cold War, 100
collaboration, 86–87
  communication, curation and, 89–122
  elitism and, 146–47
  Information Age necessitating, 16
  self-actualization in context of, 17
  Southwest Airlines example of, 126–27
  with Stewart, 109–10
colleges and universities
  branded colleges and, 27–28
  continuing education and, 158–59
  Fordham University, 43
  hiring practices involving top-ranking, 27–28
  Pitney Bowes University, 158
  Pixar University, 29
  presidents, 155
  University of Pennsylvania, 39
communication
  Apple-Google-Amazon-Microsoft alliances and, 107
  CEO replacement consulting client example, 93–95
  collaboration, curation and, 89–122

customer input and, 103–6
Dove campaign and, 104–5
external, 96
globalization and, 101
Hulu and, 106–7
Information Age, 84
Maslow's Hierarchy of Needs and,
    126
Pepsi Refresh, 105–6
technology, 15–16, 86
community mental health
    movement, 43
compensation
    CEO-front-line employee ratio, 148
    ego management and, 168
    elitism and, 156–57
    equity share as partial, 157
    women's earning power, 71, 72
competition
    creating unnatural, 171
    creativity inhibited by, 202
    ego gratification and, 168
    internal, 80–81, 101
    Story Idol, 31
connectors, 152
Consigliere, 195–97, 199–200
Constitution, 56
The Container Store, 49, 158–59
continuing education, 158–59
conversational media, 90–91
COO. See Chief Operations Officer
Cook, Tim, 198
Coppola, Francis Ford, 195
corporate anthropology, 11–51
    motivated skills in, 50–51
    1980s and 1990s eras and, 12–13
    prehistory society and, 11–12
    refined approach, 50
    study of corporate culture, 42

Corporate Anthropology (company).
    See also clients
    CEO replacement search
        consultation, 93–95
    early coaching projects, 45–48
    start of, 44
    start-ups as clients of, 48–49
The Cosby Show, 70
cosmetics companies, reverse
    diversity in, 141–43
Costolo, Dick, 37–38, 189–90
Cowell, Simon, 170
craftspeople, 26, 155–56, 210
creativity
    encouragement for, 181–82
    hindrances to, 137–38, 202
    Information Age, 15
crisis management, 186–87
Cross, Rob, 152
crowd sourcing, 85
culture
    closed-door, 95
    defining Beta, 1
    globalization breaking barriers of,
        86–87
    Neolithic, 57
    study of corporate, 42
Cup-a-Soup, 22
curation
    Beta career, 119–20, 158
    Beta leader, 17, 113–15
    boards of directors, 115
    communication, collaboration
        and, 89–122
    definition, 114
    Information Age, 122
customers
    on advisory boards, 106
    information required by, 98

customers (*continued*)
  listening to, 103–6
  told not sold approach to, 98, 106
  ways to engage, 129–30

de Waal, Frans, 75
decision-making
  CEO, 97–98
  changes, 154–55
  during crisis, 186–87
  ego-based, 164–65
  women compared to men, 117–18
Delivering Happiness (Hsieh), 128–29
democracy, 97
Deutsch, Bob, 117–18
DeVry Inc., 155, 174
Dickens, Charles, 1
digital publishing, 20–21
direct reports, CEO, 189
Disclosure, 70
Disney, Walt, 19, 106–7. *See also* The
  Walt Disney Company
diversity
  reverse, 141
  skill, 102
Doerr, John, 196–97
Dove, 104–5
Drake, Francis, 55
Drive (Pink), 85
Duflo, Esther, 77
Dunant, Sarah, 13
Dunne, Jimmy, 22–23
DuPont, 175

earning power. *See* compensation
e-books, 20–21
economic downturn
  of 2008, 22
  women and, 72

Edison, Thomas, 58
ego management, 27, 161–87
  compensation and, 168
  Consigliere, 192, 196
  ego defined, 161–62
  self-awareness for, 162, 164–65
Eisenhower, Dwight, 193
Eisner, Michael, 191–92
elitism, 26, 140–44
  banishing, 149, 156–57, 161
  collaboration and, 146–47
  compensation and, 156–57
  definition of, 141
  office building organization, 148
Elizabeth I, 55–56
e-mail, from "weak" executive, 180
emotional commitment, employee,
  135–38
employee development, 17–18, 32
  continuing education for, 158–59
  curation of, 158
  personalized approach to, 120–21
employee input
  Information Age and, 84–86
  Starbucks example, 101–2
employees. *See also* knowledge
  workers
  alignment of interests with Beta
    organizations, 50
  angular, 28
  CEO empowerment of, 174–75
  CEO notebook on interests of,
    114
  cherry-picked candidates from
    top-ranking colleges, 27–28
  compensation ratio of CEO to
    front-line, 148
  Disney's quality control, 135
  diversity of talent in, 102

doing well doing good approach to,
   121–22
emotional commitment of, 135–38
encouraging buy-in from, 113
as facilitators, 150–51
front-line, 148–49
ignoring input from, 82
innovative, 28–29
ownership, 101
passions of, 130
rewards, 32–33, 114
satisfaction and productivity, 29–30
unconventional, 141–43
volunteer projects sponsored for,
   121–22
employment rate, 2009, 72
Encarta, 85
Enrico, Roger, 174
entitlement, 84
entrepreneurship
   Alpha model and, 21–22
   Industrial Age "visionaries" and, 58
Eos Industries, 39
Ernst & Young, 158
European Union (EU), 117
external communication, 96

Facebook, 19–20, 33
facilitators, 150–53, 157
FAO Schwarz, 19
Fast Company, 122
FedEx, 136–37
feedback systems, 181
females. *See* Alpha females; women
The Feminine Mystique (Friedan), 67
feminists, 1960s and 1970s, 70
15 percent rule, 129
Flatiron Partners, 43
floor plans, 2–3, 4, 45, 148

Forbes, 117
Fordham University, 43
Fortune, 23, 176
   on Intuit, 121
   on Wegmans, 31–32
Fossey, Diane, 74
Frankfort, Lew, 194
Freud, Sigmund, 162
Friedan, Betty, 66, 67
front-line employees, 148–49
Fruit of the Loom, 190

Galdikas, Birutė, 74
*Games Mother Never Taught You:
   Corporate Gamesmanship for
   Women*, 12–13
Gates, Bill, 173
GEICO Insurance, 190
gender
   board quotas based on, 117
   post–World War II barriers, 67
   scientific study of definitions, 76–77
gender roles
   Agricultural Age changes in, 53–55
   career statistics and, 59
   genetic research on, 75–77
   in marriage, 40–42
   1950s, 63–64
   in prehistory societies, 52
   scientific justification for, 59–63
General Motors, 81
genetic research, 75–77
GeoCities, 48
George III, 56
Gibson, William, 42
globalization
   communication and collaboration
      necessitated by, 101
   partnerships and, 86–87

GMC. *See* Green Mountain Coffee
GMI Ratings, on women on boards
    of directors, 117
Goddesses, 54
Godfather, The 195
Goldman Sachs, 30
Goldsmith, Russell, 30–31
Goodall, Jane, 74
Goodnight, Jim, 30
Google, 29, 197
    alliances and collaborations of, 107
    Google+ compensation, 168
Google News, 29
Gore, Bill, 175–76
Graduate School of Education, 43
Grameen Bank, 77
grandmother, as Beta leader example,
    43–44
Grazer, Brian, 192–93
Great Depression, 59
Green Mountain Coffee (GMC), 130
Group Think, 85
Guardian, 14

Hackordnung, 61
Hallmark, 28
Hamburger, Daniel, 155, 181–82
Hamm, Jon, 68
hard sell, 98
Harper's Bazaar, 104
Harrington, Richard, 25–26
Heir Apparent, 197–98, 199
Hemming, Alison, 30
Hermès purse, 113
heuristic workers, 15, 137
Hierarchy of Needs, Maslow's,
    123–26
    pyramid, 26, 210
Hierarchy of Titles, pyramid, 210

High Tower Advisors, 39
hiring practices
    academic credentials and, 143
    cherry-picked candidates and,
        27–28
    ego-based, 163
    employee innovation and, 28–29
    hiring superstars, 103, 150
    Zappos, 127–28
Holden, Richard, 29
homosexuality, bonobo, 75
horizontal ambition, 36
horizontal structure, of prehistoric
    societies, 52
Howard, Ron, 192–93
Hsieh, Tony, 127–29
Hulu, 106–7
human nature, Beta model and, 35
hunter-gatherer societies, 52, 53
Hurley, Chad, 197
Huxley, Aldous, 123
hypothetical companies
    first/more traditional, 1–5
    second, 5–9

IBM, 152, 173
idea box, 113
IDEO, 138
Imagine Films, 192–93
Industrial Age, 12, 15, 57
    decision-making in, 81–82
    local and regional business in, 83
    robber barons, 58
    seniority premium in, 82
    women's work in, 59
Information Age
    CEO communication styles and,
        84
    collaboration, 16

communications technology and, 15–16
curation as ideal fit for, 122
customers and, 98
employee input and, 84–86
entitlement obsolete in, 84
facilitator role in, 151
globalization, 86–87
heuristic nature of, 15, 137
Promethean Myth of, 82
secrecy norm of, 96
years leading up to, 79
information technology, 79, 83–86
crowd sourcing, 85
social mores and, 100
Infotainment Corporation, 43
inner circle, 147
innovation, 28, 29
Intel, 145
internal competition, 80–81, 101
International Olympic Committee, 76
Internet communication
protest and, 88
secrecy disallowed by, 91
interpersonal skills, 179
Intuit, 121
isolation, CEO, 107–9

Jack Welch-style CEO. See Welch, Jack
Jackman, Toni, 74
James, LeBron, 72–73
JetBlue, 23–25
Jobs, Steve, 82, 196–97, 198
Jones, January, 68
Jordan, Michael, 99
J.P. Morgan Partners, 43
June Cleaver, 63

Keaton, Diane, 70
Kelleher, Herb, 126–27
Keller, Helen, 42
King, Stephen, 21
knowledge workers
childhood of today's, 71
highest needs achieved by, 139
treatment as principals desired by, 97
work environments sought by, 120
Kraft Foods, 83
Krakoff, Reed, 194–95
Kurzweil, Ray, 100

landscape painting, in office, 107–8
lattice organizations, 175–76
The Law of Accelerating Returns, 100
leaders. See also Alpha leaders; Beta leaders
Agricultural Age, 55
authenticity in, 96–97
authoritarian, 88
Leakey, Louis, 74
learning organization, 157, 160
Lifeline Exercise, 177–78
LinkedIn, 88
Linux Operating System, 84–85
The Lion King, 135
listening, 185
to customers, 103–6
tour, 184
Lombardi, Vince, 89
Lopez, Gerry, 96, 102, 156
Lowe's, 207

Maccoby, Michael, 27, 172
Mad Men, 68, 170
males. See men
managed ego. See ego management

management
  Beta managers, 154
  career path, 201, 206–8
  crisis, 186–87
  mushroom, 90
Manhattan Leather Bags, 194
"Mark" (CEO go-to guy), 132–33
marketing, cause-related, 205
marriage, gender roles in, 40–42
Maslow, Abraham, 26, 123–26, 210
matriarchies, bonobo, 74
Mattel, 144–46
media. *See also* social media
  conversational, 90–91
media company (hypothetical)
  advice sought by, 3–4
  digital division, 4
  headquarters, 1–3
  introducing, 1–5
  workstations, 4
men, decision-making in women
  compared to, 117–18. *See also*
  Alpha males
mental health, community, 43
microlending, 57, 77
Microsoft, 107, 173
military structure, 134
Miller, Jon, 96–98, 115, 148
  on teams, 153–54
mindfulness, 176–77
mini-sabbaticals, 28
minutes-taking, 13
Miracle Worker, 42
Missing Piece, 193–95, 199
missions
  Beta leader as establishing, 174
  teams as accomplishing, 153–54
M&Ms, 30
Modern Family, 39–40

monastery metaphor, 175
Moore, Demi, 70
Moore's law, 99–100
Morgridge, John, 149
motivated skills
  of Beta leaders, 16–17
  COO and, 207
  corporate anthropology, 50–51
Motivation and Personality (Maslow),
  123–24
MS-DOS, 173
Mundy, Liza, 72
Munger, Charlie, 190–91
mushroom management, 90
music industry, 169–70

NAFTA. *See* North American Free
  Trade Agreement
narcissism, 27, 170–73, 176
National Basketball Association
  (NBA), 72–73, 103
Neeleman, David, 23–25
Negroponte, Nicholas, 79
Neolithic cultures, 57
Netflix, 170
new economy companies, 32
New York Times, 30
The New Yorker, 194
newspaper publishing, Thomson's
  shift from, 25–26
Nietzsche, Friedrich, 52
Nordstrom, Jim, 175
North American Free Trade
  Agreement (NAFTA), 86
nursing, 59

offices. *See also* floor plans;
  organization charts
  typical Alpha, 2–3

Olympic Games, sex testing for, 76
open source methodology, 84–85
orchestra analogy, 114
    army general, 33–35
    conductor and, 165
organization charts, 7–8, 165–66
The Organization Man (Whyte), 69
organizational pyramids, 54
Orkut, 29
outdoor equipment company
    (hypothetical)
    introducing, 5–9
    new product line, 8
    organizational model, 7–8
    rural setting of, 5

Pacino, Al, 195
Page, Larry, 168
Palo Alto Research Center (PARC),
    82
Parker, Sean, 33
Parsons, Richard, 196
partnerships, cross-cultural, 86–87.
    See also collaboration
passions, 130
PayPal, 202
pecking order, 61
People Operations, 29
Pepsi, 174
Pepsi Refresh, 105–6
personal lives, Beta model in,
    39–40
*Personality and Social Psychology
    Bulletin*, 168
personalized approach
Peter Principle, 111
physical strength, 58
physiological needs, 124, 125
Pink, Daniel, 85

Pitney Bowes University, 158
Pixar, 28–29
Pixar University, 29
plow, invention of, 52–53
post-war era, gender barriers, 67
Pottruck, David, 38–39
prehistory, 11–12
    gender roles in, 52
    horizontal structure of, 52
presidents
    college and university, 155
    vice-presidential candidates, 195
primates, 61–62
    contemporary study of, 74–75
productive narcissists, 27, 173
productivity, 29–30
Promethean Myth, 82
promotions, negative side of, 155
protest, Internet communication and,
    88
Providence Equity Partners,
    106–7
psychological satisfaction, 130–31
purse, Hermès, 113
pyramid
    Hierarchy of Needs, 26, 210
    Hierarchy of Titles, 210
    organizational, 54
    silos created by, 80, 81
    structure, 79–82

razor and blades business model,
    20
recording industry, 169
Red Eagle Ventures, 38–39
Redbox, 170
reverse diversity, 141–43
revolutions, 64–65
    1970s and 1980s, 15

rewards
  craftspeople, 155–56
  employee, 32–33, 114, 155–56
The Richer Sex (Mundy), 72
Right Hand, 189–93
risk-taking, 138
robber barons, 58
Rockefeller, John D., 58
Roman Empire, 54, 183
Rorschach test, 108
Rosen, Sherri (hypothetical CEO),
  3, 4–5
Rosie the Riveter, 59, 60, 63
R.R. Donnelley, & Sons Company,
  43

safety needs, 124, 125
"Sam," 36–37
Sandler O'Neill & Partners, 22–23
Sarah (client), 202–4
Sarbanes-Oxley Act (SOX), 115–16
SAS, 29–30
satisfaction, 29–30, 130–31
Schjelderup-Ebbe, Thorleif, 60–61
Schmidt, Eric, 197
Schultz, Howard, 101–2, 174
Schwab, Charles, 38–39
science
  biology and gender, 77
  gender roles justified by, 59–63
  genetic research, 75–77
  primate studies, 62, 74–75
  social, 77
secrecy
  Alpha model and, 90–91, 96
  closed-door culture, 95
self-actualization, 209
  company, 18
  definition of, 17

employee opportunities for,
  138
in Maslow's Hierarchy of Needs,
  123–26
shift required for, 26
self-awareness
  COO career decision example of,
    37–38
  ego management through, 162,
    164–65
self-esteem, 125
  Alpha model as decreasing,
    131
  Dove Self-Esteem Fund, 104
sense of entitlement, 84
September 11 attacks, 22, 23–25
Serve-a-palooza, 121
sex testing, Olympic Games, 76
Sharkey, Tina, 162
silo effect, 80, 81
skills
  diverse, 102
  interpersonal, 179
  motivated, 16–17, 50–51, 207
  soft, 151
Slap, Stan, 136
Sloan, Alfred, 81
Smartphone, 91
Smith, Fred, 136–37
Smith, Greg, 30
Smith, Walter Bedell, 193
snacks, 22, 30
social interactions, Alpha model
    impact on, 64
social media
  CEO dismissing, 172–73
  customer advisory boards through,
    106
  policies, 92

protest networks through, 88
Zappos use of, 128
social mores, 100
social network analysis, 152
social science, gender and, 77
soft sell, 98
soft skills, 151
South African companies, women on
boards in, 117
Southwest Airlines, 126–27
SOX. *See* Sarbanes-Oxley Act
Spanish Armada, 55
sports, 103
Standard Oil, 58
Starbucks, 101–2, 156, 174
start-ups, 32
as Corporate Anthropology clients,
48–49
org charts, 165–66
Zappos example, 127–29
steam engine, 57–58
Stewart (co-worker pseudonym),
109–10
Stewart, Martha, 13
Story Idol competition, 31
storytelling, 30–31
stress, testosterone and, 77
success
Alpha model judgment of, 131–32
spotting companies and, 159–60
variations allowed for in Beta
model, 119–20
Sullivan, Annie, 42, 44, 51
superstars, 103, 150
Survivor, 48
Swartz, Jeffrey, 121, 122

Tahrir Square, 88
Talk Line, Butterball Turkey, 98–99

Tan, Amy, 21
teamwork
missions as accomplished by,
153–54
outdoor equipment company
support team, 8
at Pixar, 29
self-directed, 176
sports example, 103
Story Idol for promoting, 31
thanking team members for
successful, 180
technology. *See* communication;
information technology
tenure, 107
Tesla, Nikola, 58
testosterone, stress and, 77
Thiel, Peter, 202
Thomson Corporation, 25–26
Thomson Reuters, 25–26
3M, 129
Tiananmen Square, 88
Timberland, 49, 121–122
Time Warner, 196
TMP Worldwide, 43
The Today Show, 24, 104
told not sold approach, 98, 106
Tommy Hilfiger, 194
top performers, 150
Toynbee, Polly, 14
tribal councils, 166–67
Twitter, 88
CEO stepping down, 37–38
former COO, 37–38
Right Hand, 189–90

undercover boss, 159, 182–83
Underhill, Paco, 71–72
Union Square Ventures, 84

universities. *See* colleges and
  universities
UVN, 173

Valentine's Day 2007, JetBlue delays
  on, 24–25
vice-presidential candidates, as
  Missing Pieces, 195
Vietnam War, 188
Vogue, 104
volunteer projects, 121–22

W. L. Gore and Associates, 175–76
Wachner, Linda, 13
Wade, Dwyane, 73
Wall Street Journal, 19
Walsingham, Francis, 55
The Walt Disney Company, 191–92
  quality control employee from, 135
Warhol, Andy, 100
Warnaco, 13
Washington, George, 186–87
The Washington Post, 29
web sites, number of, 91
Wegman, Robert, 32
Wegmans, 31–32, 137
Weight Watchers, 105
Welch, Jack, 14–15, 99
Wells, Frank, 191–92
West Point, 134
Westinghouse, George, 58
Wharton School of Business, 39
Whinfrey, Helen, 121
Whole Foods, 176
Whyte, William H., 69
Wikipedia, 85
Williams, Evan, 37–38, 189
Wilson, Fred, 84, 97, 118, 156–57

Wolfe, Tom, 69
women
  achievements, 71
  apprenticeships denied, 46
  board of directors quotas, 117
  on boards of directors, 116–18
  decision-making in men compared
    to, 117–18
  earning power of, 71, 72
  economic downturn resilience of,
    72
  exclusion of, 56–57
  facilitators as, 151
  Great Depression and, 59
  Industrial Age professions
    available to, 59
  in Neolithic cultures, 57
  1960s and 1970s feminists, 70
  Women's Movement rebirth, 67
work stations. *See* floor plans
Work-Life department, 203–4
workplace
  evolution and transformation of,
    204
  work environment sought by
    knowledge workers, 120
workweek, thirty-five hour, 203
World Trade Center, 22–23
World War II, 59–60, 66–67, 159

Xerox, 82

Yahoo, 48
YouTube, 88
Yunus, Muhammad, 77

Zappos, 127–29
Zhang, Liqing, 168